George Tremlett has been a rock writer almost since the music began in the mid-Fifties. He left King Edward VI School, Stratford-upon-Avon, in 1957 and then spent four years on *The Coventry Evening Telegraph* writing their daily TV column and reviewing all the visiting pop package shows.

In 1961 he moved to London and became a freelance writer, working part-time for *The New Musical Express*. He has since been London correspondent for TV and pop music magazines in Japan, Holland, Sweden, the United States, Belgium, Germany, Australia, New Zealand and Finland. In this he is partnered by his wife, Jane. They also contribute to most major British teenage magazines.

Outside pop music journalism, George Tremlett pursues a political career as a member of the Greater London Council. For the past eleven years he has also been a councillor in Richmond-upon-Thames.

Also by George Tremlett

THE DAVID BOWIE STORY
THE OSMOND STORY
THE ROLLING STONES STORY
THE GARY GLITTER STORY
THE SLADE STORY

George Tremlett

The David Essex Story

Futura Publications Limited

A Futura Book

First published in Great Britain in 1974
by Futura Publications Limited
Reprinted 1975

Copyright © George Tremlett Limited 1974

This book is sold subject to the condition that it shall not,
by way of trade or otherwise, be lent, re-sold, hired out or
otherwise circulated without the publisher's prior consent in
any form of binding or cover other than that in which it is
published and without a similar condition including this
condition being imposed on the subsequent purchaser.

ISBN 0 8600 7094 8
Printed in Great Britain by
Hazell Watson & Viney Ltd
Aylesbury, Bucks

Futura Publications Limited
49 Poland Street
London W1A 2LG

ACKNOWLEDGEMENTS

This book is largely based on my own interviews with David Essex over the past four years, and I am also grateful to his manager Derek Bowman for so kindly making his own records available to me, and filling in many of the gaps. Thanks are also due to Anglo-EMI who supplied the cast lists, synopses and biographical information on those connected with David's two major films *That'll Be The Day* and *Stardust* which I have reproduced in the appendices so that all David's fans will have a lasting record of his work.

CHAPTER ONE

The basic ingredient of most show business success stories is the climb from rags to riches. It was so in the late Victorian and Edwardian heyday of British music hall and American vaudeville, and continued to be so as this slowly gave way to the movie era through the twenties, thirties and forties, and it has remained so during the fifties, sixties and now the seventies as television and the recording industry have become the main sources of public entertainment. It's a simple fact, a certain tradition; most artistes have been and still are of working class background. So it would be understandable to think of David Essex as just another docker's son made good. But his story is much more interesting than that.

Like the rest of his generation, like Jim Maclaine, the character he portrays in the films *That'll Be The Day* and *Stardust*, David grew up collecting records and listening to Elvis Presley, Little Richard, Bill Haley and all the other mid-fifties American rock 'n' roll stars; he, too, started to play an instrument and graduated to teenage groups before taking to the road with amps in the back of a van. But there the parallel ends. Back in 1964, David Essex jumped off the rock 'n' roll waggon. And he did so because of one man, Derek Bowman, who discovered him that year, when he admits he knew very little about the music business. But Bowman did understand the more traditional ways of the theatre, being a journalist, writing theatrical notes for *The Sunday Telegraph*, a paper that is as close to rock 'n' roll as pig farming is to the aeronautical industry. It was an unlikely partnership, but from the moment they met Derek Bowman was convinced that David Essex was a star. And that faith was to surmount every disappointment until eventually David did become one – eight years later.

It's an extraordinary story; faith is usually very one-sided in the music business – the artistes have it when no-one else does, and lack of recognition breaks many of their hearts along the way. But here was a partnership, founded on that faith – and however miserable and depressed David Essex may have felt as one failure followed another, as eight solo discs flopped, as the duo David and Rozaa sank almost without trace, as he switched from one recording company to another, as he missed the lead in the film *The Boy Friend*, there was the ever-constant Derek Bowman telling him all the time that he really was a star, and that it was only a matter of time before other people realised this, too.

Bowman proved to be more than just a shoulder to cry on. When David collapsed with bronchitis, it was Bowman who suggested that he move into repertory and work as an actor – and it was Bowman who suggested that he learn to dance and tap dance so that he could also appear in musical productions, who secured him a season as Tommy Steele's understudy at the London Palladium, who negotiated him a season in pantomime in Manchester. Later, when David was out of work drawing unemployment money at the Labour Exchange with his wife pregnant and a mortgage to pay, it was Derek Bowman who said. 'Don't give up now – you're a star!' And he meant it; he always had.

Like all good show business stories, there was a fairy-tale ending. David was one of two thousand hopefuls who auditioned for parts in the London stage production of *Godspell* – and was offered the lead role, playing Jesus as a red-nosed clown. It became the most talked-about London show of 1972, with even Harold Hobson in *The Sunday Times* comparing David's performance with that of Laurence Olivier. The film offers followed, and the one that David and Derek chose was *That'll Be The Day*, chronicling the story of Jim Maclaine, a fictional pop singer. No-one really expected it, but the film became one of the top box office successes of 1973 – and David went on to make the follow-up, *Stardust*, in the spring of 1974. Meanwhile, he signed a five-year recording contract with CBS Records with six figure advances, and in August, 1973, released his first CBS single *Rock On* which went to Number One in the British charts the following month, and reached Number One in the US charts in March, 1974, selling a total of over 2,000,000 copies world-wide. David followed this with another hit single, *Lamplight*, and then a third, *America*. All three singles he had written himself, just as he also wrote seven of the tracks on his first album.

And thus by mid-1974, David Essex – who three years earlier had been unemployed and drawing weekly dole – found himself a Film Star, a Stage Star, a Rock Star, and a Number One Songwriter. He had become a four-dimensional success, out-flanking the other idols of his generation most of whom remain unknown outside the world of rock 'n' roll. By any standards, the David Essex story is a remarkable one.

CHAPTER TWO

David Essex has very mixed childhood memories; some of them romantic, warm and tender, and some sad. He was an only child, born on July 23rd, 1947, and christened David Albert Cook by his parents. His father, Albert Cook, was a London docker, working in the Royal group of docks, and coming from a partly Scottish and partly Yorkshire background, which was in itself unusual, for dockland tended in those days to be very clannish, with sons following fathers, one generation succeeding another, grateful to have work when other parts of the country did not and preserving it for themselves. It was an almost closed world, but the Cook family was never solely of it. David's mother, Mrs. Doris Cook (née Kemp) was the daughter of an Irish gypsy, and a great niece of the late Gypsy Rose Lee, one of the most famous Romany fortune tellers, for long known as The Queen of the Gypsies.

'His parents were very loving,' says Derek Bowman, who has known the family for over ten years since he first saw David performing with a group at an East End pub, and has been his manager ever since. 'They are very honest and high principled parents, and brought David up to be very family-conscious.'

Now, after experiencing some ill-health, Mr. Cook works as a tally clerk in the docks, though before David was born while his father was still in the Army he used to sing with different bands, and over twenty-five years ago record producer Norman Newell, who was later responsible for many of Cliff Richard's hits, worked with him in Forces concerts.

'He had a bloody good voice,' David once told me, 'but his trouble was that he couldn't face going out on stage in front of an audience.'

But that was wartime. David's own earliest memories of his father are of him coming home from work in the evenings with his shoulders bleeding after unloading sides of beef from the ships that had recently docked with their cargoes from North and South America. In those days, his mother used to supplement the family income by scrubbing floors. The family home was in a block of flats in Plaistow, one of the poorer parts of West Ham, and according to Bowman, 'a very rough and tumble area, but like all traditional working class districts one where the people had an affinity for each other, a loyalty towards their friends and neighbours, a camaraderie, though it was still very much the other side of the tracks'.

Later, the family moved to Canning Town, a very similar area, and David went to the Star Lane primary school, where he was happy though undistinguished, liking English and loving soccer. Being close to the West Ham ground, the school had a football tradition, and such famous players as John and David Charles and Frank Lampard had started playing their soccer there. The school had a family atmosphere, with the teachers often staying in the same job for many years so that children and parents came to know them closely – the sort of atmosphere in which if Dad was sent to gaol and Mum was finding life difficult, the teachers knew when to make allowances for little Johnnie. In 1973, one of David's former teachers Percy Dunlop died at the age of 87, still working at Star Lane after sixty-seven years in his profession, becoming the longest serving teacher in Britain. Likewise, David's former headmistress Miss Mary Hood retired in April, 1974, after forty-two years as a teacher, all of them in that area. It was that type of school. Just before she retired, Miss Hood was interviewed by the local newspaper *The Stratford Express*, and told them that she remembered that David 'didn't stand out. He was a very gentle little boy. I never heard him sing at school, but he has done remarkably well.'

In those early years, David used to spend his school holidays down in the hopfields and orchards of Essex and Kent, staying in their caravans with his gypsy relatives, helping gather in the harvests by day, sitting around the open fires in the evening. 'It was always very romantic,' he told me, and I knew what he meant, having sat round gypsy fires myself as a child, faces lit by the flames, billy cans of tea and coffee being passed around with the food. 'They're very good people, gypsies – the real gypsies. I felt something for them with my mother coming from that background, though we were never gypsies ourselves ... we always lived in flats or houses ... every year I used to look forward to the summer holidays, because I knew I'd be going down there again, and I'd be in the country, listening to them talking, and every time I went nothing seemed to have changed ... and then in the evening, an uncle would get out an accordion and they'd all sing traditional songs around the fire.'

The only really unhappy part of his childhood was when

his father was taken ill, and the family went through a bad time, financially – so bad that they lost their home and were put into emergency accommodation by the West Ham borough council. 'David doesn't like talking about it now,' says Bowman, but I understand that for many months while his father was in hospital and afterwards David and his mother were kept in temporary accommodation with other homeless families, each of them just living in a curtained cubicle with the most basic of furniture. 'His father is a very proud man, a fiercely independent man – and his mother is as well. Both of them are very hard working people, which must have made the experience even more hideous for them,' says Bowman. David described it thus when interviewed by the magazine *Petticoat*: 'Oh, yes I had the complete romantic beginning. Brought up in a workhouse; born the only child of a docker who got ill with TB. We were very poor and couldn't afford to live anywhere; my mum was scrubbing pubs out and looking after me, so the Council put us in the West Ham workhouse and we stayed there for eighteen months until dad came out of hospital and started to work again.'

With the family back together again, and his father once more drawing a wage in the docks, the Cooks moved to the council house in Chadwell Heath that was to be David's home until he left school at sixteen. His parents had originally had high hopes for him, educationally. In his pre-teens, David had seemed all set for a grammar school education. That was what his parents wanted, thinking that thus he would provide himself with a secure career – the very thing his father would have liked to have had. But it was not to be. David discovered that if he went to grammar school, he would have to play rugger – whereas if he went to secondary school he could play soccer. It was an important discovery for him – he had set his heart on being a professional footballer, hopefully playing for the local heroes, West Ham. And when the time came for him to complete his eleven plus examination papers, David drew a portrait of Popeye across his paper – and not surprisingly, failed. But he got his way and went to the Shipman Road County Secondary School, where he was able to carry on with his football, though to this day he is extremely scathing about the school itself.

'I was around the top of the class for the first two years I was there, and then it dawned on me that much of the work I was doing didn't seem necessary – and in the third year I got into music and playing football, and that was the end of work . . . the school was short staffed and we never had any music, art or drama lessons. All we had was bread and butter lessons, which didn't interest me very much apart from English which I enjoyed because I found reading stories exciting . . . the teachers blamed it on the company I kept, because by then I was going round with a gang, and was constantly on the verge of being expelled, especially after setting fire to the science laboratory,' says David, who has often commented that if it hadn't been for music he would probably have ended up in gaol.

In another interview, again *Petticoat*, he says: 'I definitely felt the need to find something worthwhile that I'd be happy doing; the alternatives were either working in the docks where everyone went to work, or staying on at school and trying to get GCEs, and neither of those meant much to me. I was lucky because I found a way out through music and theatre, but a lot of kids don't find it. I mean, the mates I was at school with who haven't become dockers are now mostly crooks, gangsters or car-dealers. I didn't really fancy any of that. It was all the fault of this very bad school we went to.'

Likewise, he told *The Sun* that around this time he was beaten up by a gang in the Mile End Road, and that at school 'the CID used to come round looking for weapons'. And he has also said that though setting fire to the science laboratory was bad enough, gassing the biology master's bees was regarded as even worse! 'We dismantled the bunsen burner and let the gas in, and he started smashing me with a cane,' says David.

By the time he was twelve, David was earning himself extra pocket money by selling newspapers – and every Saturday he used to go down to the Rathbone Street market, working on a fruit and vegetables stall dressed in a snazzy waistcoat, open necked shirt with a cravat around the neck, and sometimes with a golden earring. With fruit in his hand, he would wave his arms and shout: 'Apples shillin' a pahnd, tanner n'arf, they're luverlee!' or 'Nanas! Shillin' n'arf for a luvlee girl!'

'I'd chat up all the old dears into buying from me,' he says. 'I used to wear a little cheesecutter cap, smoked cigarettes that I rolled myself, and thought I was the cat's whiskers . . . my lunch used to consist of five cigarettes, sixpennorth of chips and a pickled onion . . . it was always an anti-climax when I had to go back to school afterwards.'

Then on the Saturday evenings, David would catch a Tube up to the centre of London, and wander around the Soho jazz clubs, still wearing the same loud-patterned waistcoats, and the brightly coloured cravats, looking a little like Ronnie Lane does today. In that same *Petticoat* interview, he remembered: 'The first time I was really struck by music was when I was about thirteen and I used to come up to the West End and just walk around. You know, just around the streets I'd get the feeling that it was really exciting. I went to the Flamingo Club about eleven o'clock one night, quite scary it was, and there was Georgie Fame's band and I couldn't believe how good it sounded. I'd already started messing around on the drums and I decided then I wanted to be a jazz drummer. The other things like singing I got sort of side-tracked into, but music in general was the main driving force early on.'

Still at school, football was the governing passion of his life – and he says that though a poor scholar his teachers had a soft spot for him because he did at least throw all his energies into every game of soccer, eventually playing for the school, and then for West Ham Boys at left half. It was an area where the schools attached great importance to sports, and in his two-part BBC TV schools programme in February, 1974, David explained: 'They've got a really good football team here. In 1973 they won the Newham Primary Cup Final. Football and boxing thrive in this kind of area. It's a way of getting out of your environment, getting famous, making some money. But most of the kids won't become professional footballers or boxers.'

Malcolm Allison, later to become manager of Manchester City and more recently the Crystal Palace team, used to coach the West Ham Boys' team at that time, it being the club's policy to encourage teenagers to work their way up through the club with the ultimate dream of making the first team. 'He liked David a lot,' Derek Bow told me, 'but because of his smoking David found he wasn't quick enough on the ball, and that told against him a bit ... when I first met him in 1964 when he was seventeen, he was smoking about twenty cigarettes a day ... but for that, I think he might have made a career in football, playing for one of the professional clubs. He was certainly a very keen footballer, and a regular and enthusiastic supporter of West Ham.'

But this was not to be. Music had also caught his imagination, and his parents encouraged him in this just as they had always sought to help David make the most of himself; although in the many times he and I have spoken, he has seemed reluctant to talk about his childhood and his family, it is clear that Mr. and Mrs. Cook were devoted parents, providing their son with a happy home. This emerges in the occasional anecdote he relates. Once we were talking fairly close to Christmas, and the conversation turned to memories of Christmas past. Smiling, David told me that Father Christmas had kept on calling at his home long after he did at the other houses and flats in the neighbourhood. When he was ten years old, David remembered that 'our chimney had been blocked off, but I was still fairly confident that Father Christmas wouldn't forget me, and might come in through the window – so I left him a pillowcase by the window, and when I went down next morning there were apples and oranges and a pair of toy skates. When I found them – which was immediately after my parents left the room because I was lying there with my eyes shut tight – I just went berserk. I tried them out in the bedroom and nearly knocked myself unconscious ...

when my mother came into the room to see me later on that night, she found me fast asleep in bed with a smile on my face – with the skates still trussed to my feet! Next morning, I must have driven the neighbours mad because we were living in a second floor flat and I spent much of the day skating around the flat and falling over.'

The neighbours also had much to complain about when David discovered the other big thing in his life after football – the drums. On those Saturday night trips up to Soho, he had often stood at the back of the Flamingo, listening to Georgie Fame and the other bands that played there. Fame, of course, was an outstanding pianist and organist – and it was now very much the age of the lead guitar. But for David, the fascination was always watching the drummers. Later he was to idolise the American drummer Buddy Rich – and eventually he persuaded his father to buy him a snare drum that was lying in a junk shop window for 32s 6d. And for the first year or two, not being in a group or having anywhere to rehearse, he used to pound away at his one little snare drum in the flat in time to the singles on his record player – while the people living in the flat below were pounding their ceiling with a broom!

CHAPTER THREE

During the evenings while he was still attending the Shipman Road County Secondary School in Custom House by day, David used to go down regularly to the youth club organised by the Dockland Settlement, a charity patronised by Princess Margaret which David has since been keen to help financially through his work as an artiste. But in those days he was just another East End teenager who might have been drifting the streets and getting into trouble with the law, but for the club; instead, he would walk in there, listen to records, sit around the coffee bar, play billiards and snooker and the odd game of darts – and soon he started to learn some of the techniques of drumming from a professional musician who had worked in the Sidney Lipton band, and spent his spare evenings down at the club encouraging youngsters who wanted to move on from just listening to juke box records to making their own music. The lessons continued after David had left school and started an apprenticeship as a toolmaker at Plessey's electronics components factory in Ilford.

It was while he was there that he saw an advertisement in a local paper saying that a dance band needed a drummer. He replied and got the job, and found himself working as a semi-professional musician for the first time – though the engagement was short lived because he was not happy playing waltzes, quick steps and the occasional hokey cokey. So he started auditioning for groups instead –

which was how he came to join The Everons, who used to play regularly in an upstairs room at the Eagle public house in Chobham Road, London, E.15 (the Stratford/Leytonstone area) which was where Derek Bowman heard them – and David – for the first time.

'I was then living out at Harlow in Essex, but I had friends in the Wanstead area,' says Derek, who was then a freelance film and theatre news reporter retained by *The Sunday Telegraph*. 'My job was to keep in touch with producers, directors and actors, but I had few contacts with the pop music business, which I knew very little about.

'A friend of mine, Stanley Murray, who had his own cooperage business making barrels, was having dinner with me one night, and said that a boy who worked in his factory was playing in a group that was even better than the Beatles, and he asked whether I would like to see them with a view to becoming their manager jointly with him. I said, "No," and he asked me, "What have you got to lose?"

'As we discussed the matter, I was persuaded and we went down to The Eagle to see the Everons, having a drink together downstairs in the bar ... I could hear them playinng upstairs, and I can remember turning to him and saying, "It sounds good" ... then we went upstairs and stood at the back of the room listening to them play.'

The group comprised Sandra Mundy, who was then sixteen years old and had flaxen hair and played bass guitar, and lived at Earlham Grove, Forest Gate, with her nineteen years old brother Brian who was the rhythm guitarist. Sandra's fiancé John Kneller, who was eighteen and lived in Church Road, Leyton, was the lead guitarist – and there on drums was David, who then called himself Dave Cook, and was by now seventeen years old.

'They knew I was coming, and were looking very nervous,' Bowman remembers. 'I asked them to carry on playing, and they went straight into some rhythm 'n' blues numbers, about which neither my friend nor I knew too much . . . as soon as they started again, our eyes went straight to the drummer . . . he had tremendous style in the way he played drums, and very striking blue eyes . . . and he played the drums in an arrogant, throw-away style that was fascinating to watch. Immediately, I was quite stunned by his personality.'

Afterwards, Bowman returned to Stanley Murray's house and said then: 'I think Dave Cook could be an enormous star.' Bowman and Murray formed a partnership, and signed the Everons to a management contract, Susan Hampshire, a friend of Bowman, suggested that they change their name to the China Plates (which was Cockney rhyming slang for 'mates'). With his lack of knowledge of the intricacies of music business management, Derek Bowman thought he would invite down friends in the theatre and films to see what they thought of his new discovery – already looking more impressive as he fitted out Sandra Mundy in a new outfit specially designed by Mary Quant, with a hairstyle by Vidal Sassoon (both of whom were taken down to The Eagle to see the group play).

One night he invited film star Peter O'Toole and his wife Sian Phillips to go down to The Eagle, and they turned up in their Rolls Royce. 'Peter sat there at the edge of the room with his head in his hands, listening to them play . . . and was struck by David . . . he said they were very endearing and he thought their music was strong, he thought that as a group they had something special . . . a sort of "Our Gang" feeling.'

He also invited down the actresses Ann Todd and Susan Hampshire, who was later to become an internationally known TV star through her series *The Forsyte Saga*, *The Churchills* and *The Pallisers*. 'Ann was wild about them especially David and Susan liked them – and some time later she proposed David for membership of Equity,' Bowman told me.

At the time, Bowman cut some demos with the group – including two tracks *Carol Ann* and *You Got To Work*, which he still has, and which he played to me very recently. These were recorded in 1964, and sound distinctly in the Rolling Stones/Pretty Things/early Kinks/Downliners Sect idiom – with David now handling the vocals, and sounding slightly Jagger-ish. Bowman played the demos to the Beatles' recording manager George Martin, who turned them down – as did Peter Sullivan who was then in the artistes and repertoire department at Decca, working closely with Tom Jones and his manager Gordon Mills.

'Peter came down to The Eagle, but he just didn't like the group,' says Bowman. 'But he did say, "Take that boy away from the drums and put him in front of the mike – and then contact me again!" I then took the demos to George Martin at EMI, who liked the sound but thought they were just average . . . I mentioned the drummer, but he said he didn't want to see the drummer because he was having enough problems with another drummer at that time.'

It is possible that they were all searching in the wrong direction – the rhythm 'n' blues that David was recording at the time were certainly of above average standard; their quality stands up even now, even though some of the drumming is a bit frantic. But Bowman didn't really know which way to go – and when the agent/manager/impressario Bunny Lewis said he had found a great song for David to record, they did just that, even though it was quite unlike anything David had done before.

By then Stanley Murray was beginning to have problems finding enough spare time to devote to the group, and he decided with Derek Bowman that they should dissolve their managerial partnership. 'His wife was starting to say that she didn't like him being out every night with a bloody pop group, and she thought it wasn't right for a man of his age with his own business, and so on – which was very understandable . . . she wanted him to be at home in the evenings, sitting with her and watching TV, which I could understand with him being out running his business all day . . . we got to the point where he said he couldn't carry on, and the group split up around the same time, and David started his solo career . . . and that was the time when Stanley and I dissolved our agreement.'

This was in December, 1964. Dave Cook gave up an engineering apprenticeship, stayed with Bowman as sole manager – and Bowman changed his name to David Essex. 'He couldn't stay on as Dave Cook or David Cook because there was already an actor registered with Equity with that name, so we chose Essex – because that was where he came from and I also liked it because it had "sex" in it!

'David was really a "shout" singer then – the sort of

material he liked was the Ray Charles song *What'd I Say?*, and numbers by Sonny Boy Williamson, Muddy Waters and Howling Wolf, and he was very into the early Beatles and Rolling Stones ... it was mainly blues-style stuff, the sort of songs that Long John Baldry was singing at the time – which didn't seem natural for a singer who was in his teens and white! Bunny Lewis had looked after Craig Douglas's career, and what impressed him most about David was his looks ... Lewis had this record production company, and he signed David to a contract, and told us he had just the right song, *And The Tears Came Tumbling Down*, which was written by Perry Ford of the Ivy League, who were very big at that time. Lewis chose this song. It was a ballad, and I thought it was a lovely song – though David had never sung a ballad before and looking back now it does seem very unfair on him.

'We recorded it at the old Olympic studios off Blandford Street, W1, and when we went into the studio there was a thirty-five piece orchestra – with a twenty-piece string section. David had never sung with any line-up larger than the Everons before, and we both nearly fainted when we saw all these musicians in the studio. I was petrified. I felt a great responsibility towards David, and by now I knew his parents well and we had all become good friends ... then all of a sudden I became very aware of my inadequacies ... the arrangement was lovely, but looking back now I know that he just wasn't ready at that time to cope with a big ballad ... and because we had so few contacts, and I knew so little about the business, we just couldn't get any TV on that record.'

The record was released on Phillips' Fontana label in

April, 1965, and that month their press department issued the first ever David Essex press release:

> 'David Essex is a Cockney who now lives in the county from which he takes his stage name, but his family tree has colourful and international roots.
>
> 'He is a great-great-nephew of the famous fortune teller, Gipsy Rose Lee. His mother is of Irish-Spanish gipsy parentage, and his father is a Cockney of part-Yorkshire and part-Scottish descent. Born in Plaistow, East London, on 23rd July, 1947, David now lives in Dagenham, the home town of singer Sandie Shaw.
>
> 'A former apprentice mechanical engineer, David started singing as a member of a rhythm 'n' blues group, in which he played drums. Most of their experience was gained working in pubs in London's East End and Ilford, and it was at a public house in Stratford that show business writer Derek Bowman discovered him in the autumn of 1964. Originally the plan was for Derek to become manager of the group but the difficulties encountered in launching a new group were so great that the venture had to be discontinued. Nevertheless David decided to give up drumming and become a solo singer under Derek's supervision.
>
> 'Contacts in show business started drifting down to the East End to hear David working. Film star Peter O'Toole hailed him as a star of the future. Actress Ann Todd also called in to see him one night, and was so impressed that she telephoned disc jockey

Alan Freeman who recommended David to agent and disc producer Bunny Lewis.

'Lewis caught up with David when he sang at an actor's party, liked the young singer's style and decided to record him. Bunny's plans to look for a song for David during a visit to American were forestalled by Perry Ford, one of the hit-making Ivy League, who came up with a number called *And The Tears Came Tumbling Down*, which together with another Ford-penned number *You Can't Stop Me from Loving You* became David's first Fontana disc release on TF 559.

'The son of a tally clerk at London Docks, David once played soccer for West Ham School Boys. He is 5ft. 10½ins tall, weighs 11st 10lbs, has blue eyes and dark brown hair. He is a great admirer of drummer Joe Morello, and also likes Buddy Greco, John Lee Hooker, Keely Smith, Art Blakey, Jimmy Smith and Johnny Dankworth.'

The record received some radio plays, none at all on television – and less than ecstatic reviews in the British weekly music papers: –

'Two songs by Perry Ford of the Ivy League. David does a big-voiced performance on the interesting but slightly repetitive song. String-section backing mostly. A good disc all round.'
– *Record Mirror*

'Good but boring.'
– *Penny Valentine, Disc and Music Echo*

> 'Raucous, thumping beat, chanting girls and strings almost envelop the singer. But the tune is quite melodic.'
>
> – *New Musical Express*

At home, David was now practising on a £280 drum kit that his parents had bought him hoping that this would further his career, but he and Bowman were now thinking that his future lay in a solo recording career; over the next eighteen months he had three further singles released by Fontana – and only one of them was in any way successful. That was his second single *Can't Nobody Love You/Baby I Don't Mind*, which came out in December, 1965, with the A-side – which had been taken from a Moody Blues album – going to Number 17 in the Radio London chart. This too, was promoted with another press release from Philips. (Slightly exaggerated, says Bowman):

> 'Peter O'Toole, who speaks with some authority on the subject, had a few things to say about star quality when he met singer David Essex in an East End pub.
>
> ' "You are," he told the slightly overawed eighteen-year-old Cockney singer, "a natural star of the future. Actors go to school to gain naturalness and star quality. You've already got it."
>
> 'That Mr O'Toole was not making an empty prediction is evident after hearing David holler a spirited blues-influenced vocal over a moody, brassy accompaniment of *Can't Nobody Love You* on Fontana TF 620, released on December 3.

'The filmstar had been invited to watch the handsome young singer in action by David's manager, showbusiness writer Derek Bowman. Word got around and other personalities dropped by, including actress Ann Todd, who told disc jockey Alan Freeman, who told agent Bunny Lewis, who decided to put David on record.

'While waiting for his big break, David – a descendant of the famous fortune-teller Gipsy Rose Lee – spends part of his time working as a window cleaner. But once a week he attends RADA (the Royal Academy of Dramatic Art) where he takes lessons in hand-movement and he is also studying dancing.'

This single prompted writer and broadcaster Peter Noble to tip David for stardom in 1966, and attracted several favourable reviews: –

'New voice on the scene. A James Mitchell song and some way out wailing from the voice itself. Maybe it's a bit too violent to make much progress.'
– *Record Retailer*
'This new boy is really wild, selling with bluesy feel and stacks of originality. Very good.'
– *Record Mirror*

But in retrospect, it is clear that David Essex and Derek Bowman were still not quite sure of their direction; David was still very much into the solid, earthy rhythm 'n' blues sound – Derek was keen that he should learn stage presentation and how to dance. But by now David was starting to get occasional mentions in the teenage magazines, and even had his own fan club which was started by his cousin Eileen Watson among fellow-pupils at the Stratford Grammar School.

'On that record, David sang a sort of "shout" blues, but unfortunately it was given rather a straw hat backing,' says Bowman. 'This was compelling, but not quite right – though it was very popular with the pirate radio stations ... on Radio London, the disc jockey Paul Kay picked it as his record of the week, and it went to Number 17 in their chart. I was over at David's house when he heard that come through on the radio, and he danced all round the room ... he really thought he was just about to make his break-through that week ... but when the other charts came out, the record wasn't mentioned.'

For his third single, which was released on March 25th, 1966, David worked with the American singer J. J. Jackson, who had written and produced for the Shangri-Las, and had worked at the Tamla Motown organisation in Detroit, which had become the fountainhead of American black music with Martha and the Vandellas, Stevie Wonder, Marvin Gaye, the Supremes, the Miracles and since then, the Jackson Five. With Jackson as his producer, David recorded the Ray Charles classic *This Little Girl Of Mine*, with a throbbing bass line, and a Raelets-style vocal backing. Derek Bowman preferred the B-side, *Brokenhearted*, which was a revival of a Johnnie Ray hit. But the record flopped like the two previous ones.

David's final Fontana single, released on August 19th, 1966, was one that he still remembers with embarrassment. It was titled *Thigh High/De Boom Lay Boom* – and the

A-side was all about a girl walking down the Kings Road in a miniskirt. 'We pleaded with them not to release it,' says Bowman. 'But Lewis was the producer, he had the right to release it, and our pleas went unheard. Eighteen months had now gone by since David had signed with Lewis's production company Ritz Records, and we hadn't had a hit so Lewis agreed to let him go. We always got on well with him and his wife Janique, and the parting was amicable. He has since congratulated David on his more recent success.'

In spite of their four record flops, Derek Bowman's faith that David Essex was destined to be a star was still as firm as ever; the only reason he wanted a release from the Lewis contract was so that they could switch to another recording company where he thought David might be more successful. By now, David was starting to get a backing group together – he did some gigs with a group called The Anzaks, and then later toured both here and on the Continent backed by an eight-piece Stevenage group Mood Indigo.

Bowman's faith would occasionally be reinforced by comments by other artistes. One night, Derek took David down to the Cool Elephant Club, where Dudley Moore was playing piano – and David went up on stage and sang *Fly Me To The Moon* and *I'll Remember April* with Moore's accompaniment. Afterwards Bowman asked his opinion, and Dudley said: 'Yeah – tell him to keep at it!' Lionel Blair was also in the club at the time, and he came up to David afterwards and said: 'Whatever you do, never lose that huskiness in your voice.'

But encouragements like this were few and far between

– and became even more infrequent as David started touring with Mood Indigo for £30 a night, which had to be split eight-ways after their agent had taken his ten per cent, after they had paid for their petrol and repairs to their group van, and after they had made their weekly hire purchase instalments on their equipment. Quite often David would be left with just thirty shillings a week for himself – after travelling all over the country between gigs, sometimes snatching just a few hours' sleep in the back of the van.

CHAPTER FOUR

While he was still trying to find the right backing group, David Essex gave a one-man concert at the Jeanetta Cochrane Theatre in London – because both he and Bowman wanted to see how far his RADA lessons and his learning to dance had advanced his overall technique as a performer.

'That concert showed that he was acquiring an enormous amount of stage style, and I was impressed by the way he performed . . . he was acquiring control and economy, which are so important to an actor, but much rarer qualities among musicians. David had these both in plenty, and I could see that he was ready to develop his career in other ways . . .'

In this and in other ways, it was an uncertain period; both David and Derek and Bunny Lewis had been puzzled at the failure of each of those four records. 'Lewis suggested we change his name . . . I had always liked Essex because it had a good ring to it, because it was where he lived, and because it had "sex" in it, but we discussed quite seriously another name . . . he thought of calling himself David Kemp, because that was his mother's maiden name, and he also thought of David Blue . . . and we even considered quite seriously recording under the name of Stormy Tempest, because there had been so many other vaguely similar names that had been successful . . . we both thought that had a bit of class, and David liked it.

Then four years after that David was thinking of changing his name to Wellington Boot! Things were going so badly for him that he thought there must be something wrong with his name.

'These things are difficult to understand when you are successful; but when you are not succeeding and you are throwing everything you have got into your career, it's understandable to search around for explanations, and it's funny how many people look first at the name.

'Friends would come up to us, trying to be helpful, and say: "What a bad name. Why don't you change it?" And yet when you're successful then people – the same people – will tell you what a wonderful name you have chosen. It was the same with Engelbert Humperdinck – he had no success at all under his real name Gerry Dorsey, and then he changed his name and luck intervened . . . We really thought that we might have to do the same thing.'

These doubts continued while David gradually organised himself, finding the right group to work with, Mood Indigo, and signing a new five year contract with another company, MCA Records, where Mike Leander was head of production. His intention was to launch MCA as an independent company in this country – it was already well established in the United States as part of the vast Music Corporation of America. Bowman approached him almost a year before he was ready for this launch – but Leander liked the sound of David's records, asked to see him, and then signed him.

From his work with Decca where he had been a producer and arranger, working with Marianne Faithfull, The Applejacks, Billy Fury, Karl Denver, etc., Leander already had a reputation – which he had reinforced by writing hits like *Lady Godiva* for Peter and Gordon and *I've Been a Bad, Bad Boy* for Paul Jones, by creating his own orchestra, and handling arrangements, one of which was *She's Leaving Home* for the Beatles' much-praised *Sergeant Pepper* album. And it was this same number that was his first production with David Essex. The single was not released in Britain – but was rushed out in the United States on the UNI label. To promote it, Bowman himself mailed press releases to 188 American newspapers; but still the record flopped.

Around the same time, David made his film debut in *A Smashing Time*, which starred Rita Tushingham and Lynn Redgrave. 'He was supposed to be a swinging Londoner whom they kept bumping into – in the GPO Tower and in a London art gallery. It was quite a nice little part for him in theory, but it turned out to be hardly more than a walk-on,' says Bowman.

But this was just an interlude between his touring of clubs and ballrooms, which was becoming increasingly hazardous because David and Mood Indigo (who rarely earned more than £30 a night) had an agent who kept booking them into venues at opposite ends of the country on successive nights so that they were spending most of their lives in the van, and were being rapidly worn out by the strain of it. Sometimes they would be exhausted even before that night's show began – and because they had so little money coming in they had to rely on a van which kept breaking down when they were driving through the night after gigs. It was a working atmosphere in which anything and everything would go wrong at times – one night they were appearing on stage, switched on the amplification equipment, and out came the BBC News over the loudspeakers. 'How that happened, I shall never know,' says David.

'Our main trouble was the bookings – this agent used to have us playing gigs two hundred miles apart, and as I was paying the other members of the group and was responsible for all our travelling expenses, there was never enough money left over for me . . . for three weeks I never saw a bed,' David recalled. 'I was sleeping in the van, going out night after night without getting proper food, maybe just the ocasional bag of fish and chips . . . I can remember one particular night I tried to sleep in a waiting room at Central Station, Manchester, but found that every entrance door was locked, so I spent the night wandering the streets in the rain.'

After that experience. David collapsed in Manchester with bronchitis and phoned Derek Bowman – who caught the next train up to Manchester, and brought him back to his parents' home in Chadwell Heath, where the family doctor advised a six-week total rest. 'I was very worried about him at this time,' Bowman told me. 'He had caught this severe cold which had developed into a sort of 'flu and then bronchitis, and I thought he shouldn't go back to the sort of life that he had been leading before . . . Then I saw an advertisement in *The Stage*, which is a much more theatrical kind of paper, saying that actors who could sing were wanted for a touring repertory company . . . the trouble was David wasn't a member of Equity, and it's very difficult to get into that union because naturally enough they are worried that there are already eight thousand

actors out of work every week without encouraging more
... in order to qualify for membership, you have to have
a forty-week engagement, unless you are taken on as a
probationary member by one of the theatrical companies.'

David joined the union, being proposed by Susan Hampshire (who had followed his career closely since his days with the China Plates Blues Band) and seconded by Ian McShane, and he went along to audition after answering that advertisement with much prompting from Derek Bowman. The auditions were being held at a rehearsal studio in Earls Court by Zak Matalon, who was married to the West End stage star Elizabeth Seal, and whose brother Vivian Matalon ran the Hampstead Theatre Club.

'David sang a song for Matalon at the audition, he liked him, and offered him a part in a touring production he was preparing of *The Fantasticks*, which had been presented in London, and which is still running off-Broadway after fourteen years ... It's one of those shows that is memorable for certain songs; it had *Soon It's Gonna Rain* which was very successful for Barbra Streisand, and *Try To Remember*, which is one of those numbers that just about everyone has sung at one time or another ... David was chosen to play the male lead, and he was very frightened – but very excited. Matalon's company was based at Henley-on-Thames, and the spirit within the company was extremely good ... one of the other leads was Nathan Dambuza, a Bantu actor who had played the lead in *King Kong*, the African musical that had been brought over to London, and he and Matalon both gave David every encouragement.'

Matalon's touring production opened at the Festival

Hall at Paignton, Devon, and Bowman travelled down there by train to see David's opening night performance. 'I went down full of excitement,' he says, 'because I thought that was a great opportunity for him . . . I can remember it vividly now, travelling by train along the sea front between Exeter and Torquay, with that beautiful red soil, and thinking all the time that this could be a turning-point for David . . . and then I went into the theatre and took my seat, and looked down towards the stage and there were only about twenty people – yes, an audience of just twenty people . . . it was a production where the cast were introduced at the beginning of the show, and they all came on and sat facing the audience, which they very nearly outnumbered . . . David was the first to come on, and he sat down at a table, looking nervous and slightly embarrassed – he must have seen me because I was surrounded by empty seats – and he started to perpetrate a few howlers, but that didn't worry me because I'd already told him that the best way to learn to act was to make your mistakes in public – it's great for you even if it's not so great for the public.

'Actually, it was a beautiful little show and it was very sad to see so few people there . . . David sang a duet of *Soon It's Gonna Rain*, and played drums in another number. I stayed overnight so that I could see him after the show, and told him he was very good – and he was pleased that I thought so. He has always been receptive to anything I have had to say, and I knew that words of encouragement were vital to him. I told him what the mistakes were, and what qualities were definitely there, and this was what he expected me to do.'

Matalon himself was very pleased with David's performance and said so, and David made his own views known in an interview with one of the local papers in the Chadwell Heath area, *The Barking and Dagenham Post*, whom he told: 'I was a bit apprehensive at being thrown in at the deep end with all those professional actors, but I realised that you can't act properly without training. I wasn't going to do repertory work at first and I still don't think I would act on the stage again unless it was a West End part. But at the time I knew nothing about voice projection, how to work properly with the correct delivery. Now I do and it's going to help a lot.'

Bowman also asked another friend, the Australian actor Keith Michell, to go and see David in the show. Michell, a distinguished Shakespearean actor who has since had outstanding success in the BBC TV series *The Six Wives of Henry VIII*, saw the production at Henley-on-Thames, and subsequently told Bowman: 'Derek, he's marvellous.'

'Are you just saying that?' asked Bowman.

'No,' said Michell. 'He has a very natural presence on stage.'

This was very encouraging to both David Essex and Derek Bowman, and they agreed that David should appear in another repertory musical, a revival of the great Twenties stage success *Oh! Kay!* by P. G. Wodehouse and Guy Bolton, with music by George and Ira Gershwin, which had originally starred Gertrude Lawrence. Matalon cast David as the Young Duke, who spoke with a lisp. 'I was very impressed by the way he played it,' says Bowman. 'He did not entirely obliterate the Cockney accent he had ever since I had first met him, but he sounded very convincing

'... and for the first time he danced on stage ... I had been anxious that he should be a good dancer, and instead of just sending him along to any normal stage dancing school I arranged for David to take lessons from Buddy Bradley, an American negro, who was one of the best dance teachers in the world – he had taught Jessie Matthews, Audrey Hepburn and Bruce Forsyth to dance ... after he'd been to Buddy's studio in Lissom Grove a few times, Buddy told me: "You're not wasting your time with that boy." I kept getting encouragement like that from different people – and, of course, it was a great morale-booster for David to have people telling him that he would eventually get to the top.'

In this production, David appeared in costume – a well cut twenties grey suit to sing one number with the distinctly un-sixties lyric: –

> 'Stiff upper lip,
> Stout fellow,
> Carry on Old Fluff,
> Chin up,
> Keep muddling through.'

The show also had a very famous song, *Someone To Watch Over Me*, and it gave David the opportunity to develop other aspects of his talent – experience that was to come in useful, indeed prove invaluable, nearly three years later when he landed the lead role in the London stage production of *Godspell*. As an artiste, he was already maturing; when that production opened at the Princess Theatre, Torquay, the local newspaper critic in *The Tor-*

quay Herald said that he gave 'a full blooded performance.' And from there, the show moved to Southsea, Henley-on-Thames, Norwich, Southport and Salford, with David acquiring more confidence as it progressed.

'He was only earning £18 a week, but as experience it was unbeatable – much better for him than going to drama school,' says Bowman. 'He was really enoying himself even though he did feel a little like a fish out of water . . . you must realise that there is no longer any theatrical tradition among working class people. There's music hall and vaudeville, which were always working class both in the artistes and in the audiences . . . but theatre as such is now a middle class tradition, and he was very aware that he was, for the first time, appealing to middle class audiences. At this time I sent him to two very fine vocal coaches, Eric Gilder and later Harold Miller. Both thought his voice had enormous potential.'

Although he was gaining this extra experience, David still believed that success through a hit record was what he needed most – and by now MCA producer Mike Leander was ready to release his first single on MCA's UNI label. They chose a number called *Love Story*, written by Randy Newman, the American songwriter who had penned *Simon Smith And His Amazing Dancing Bear*, with a Mike Leander song *Higher Than High* on the B-side.

This was released on May 24th, 1968, and in their promotional press release MCA said that David was the first British artist to be signed to their Hollywood-based UNI label, and that 'the full character of David Essex's Country-Soul voice emerges, smoky and distinctive, through the expert production of Mike Leander. Male voices are used to enhance the unusual backing,' continuing: —

'22-year-old East Londoner DAVID ESSEX so impressed top recording producer Mike Leander that he signed him to a five-year UNI label contract twelve months before that label set up operations in Britain.

'Born in Plaistow, a few hundred yards from Bow Bells, on July 23, 1947, David is a former apprentice mechanical engineer. He started singing as a member of a Rhythm 'n' Blues group in which he was a drummer. A very powerful drummer.

'He was discovered in a pub by show business writer Derek Bowman who persuaded him to become a solo singer under his management.

'David is descended from Spanish gypsies although he grew up in East London. He once played soccer for West Ham Schoolboys. He is a trained dancer — modern jazz and tap.

'In the past eight months he has been touring Britain playing lead parts in musical comedies with a repertory company. His roles included Matt in the off-Broadway hit *The Fantasticks* and the Duke of Durham in a revival of the George and Ira Gershwin/ P. G. Wodehouse success *Oh! Kay!*

'David is an actor with the ambition to play straight film parts. Susan Hampshire and Ian McShane proposed him a member of Equity, the actors' union. He's keen to get around to producing records and directing films — but making initial impact on the

British and American charts with one of his own records is the most immediate ambition of all. With the international power of UNI behind his undoubted talents he has an obvious head-start.

'David Essex has a two-and-a-quarter octave vocal range. He can tackle blues, beat or ballads with equal facility. His many fans who have watched him in action at clubs and ballrooms up and down the country confirm that claim. But he is best known so far for his blues work with its marked coloured influence.

'This strikingly handsome singer is six foot tall, weighs eleven stone and has dark brown hair. The first thing that hits people who meet him is his pair of very, very blue eyes. "They're Botticelli blue," decided one fascinated girl student. He is mobbed by girls at all his gigs. At one venue in Staffordshire six bouncers had to escort him from the hall and the clutches of 1,000 screaming fans. And if this is the reaction he's been getting *without* the popularity boost of a hit record...

'Today David stands on the brink of his big break. When it comes he will be pleased but not overexcited. Take us up on that point six hits or six months from now. David Essex will maintain his coolest of cools.'

Such optimism, but it was all too soon. The single was not a hit, though in an indirect way it furthered his career.

CHAPTER FIVE

That single on the MCA/UNI label, *Love Story*, was the fifth that David Essex had released. This time he found himself competing with Alan Price who had also recorded the song, and for the fifth time David had a flop on his hands – though most of the BBC disc jockeys thought it would be otherwise. John Peel may have dedicated the track to his producer's tortoise, but Alan Freeman said: 'That's the version to watch. A boy with a big future, David Essex. Definite star quality there.' And Sam Costa commented that this was 'a great record and a great singer'.

The real encouragement came when Leslie Grade, probably the leading British agent and the man who had done so much to advance the career of Cliff Richard, started taking an interest in David. Bowman had been to see him with a copy of the record plus a collection of photographs, and then Leslie Grade went to see David work, and afterwards said to Bowman: 'This boy will be very big – look what we did for Cliff.' Then later, he said to Bowman: 'I've got a TV booking for you.'

'My mouth dropped when he said it, because that was the one thing we had been desperate for – a break into television . . . Leslie thought highly of David, and warned him not to rush his career but to take his time and we felt very confident that with him behind us, the break would come . . . but then Leslie had a stroke, and that was the end of that. He had to give up work for a while, and this was another great disappointment for us . . . looking back now, it's extraordinary how many major disappointments we did go through around this time.'

Around the same time, Bowman also felt that the MCA/UNI/Mike Leander tie-up was not right for David, and asked to be released from the contract.

'To put it very simply, we were hungry – and he was not,' says Derek Bowman now. 'He didn't want to rush into anything unless he was sure – and we were in a hurry because we had already had a hard struggle . . . things didn't work out quite right. David's version of *She's Leaving Home* was sent over to the States on tape, and then the record company executives in Los Angeles sat on it . . . another version of the same song was recorded by David and Jonathan with the Beatles' own record producer George Martin producing it, and that one got released before ours did, so naturally enough that was the one that got the airplay . . . we weren't happy about that . . . and then *Love Story* was a very weird record, probably very uncommercial. Leander said we would have to record something different, but this was too different – the BBC wouldn't play it! We were very upset so MCA agreed to release David from his contract after just those two records.

'Then I was walking down Oxford Street one day, and I saw Tony Macaulay walking down the other side of the street . . . I crossed the street to speak to him, and told him that we had not been happy with MCA and were getting a release, and he said, "Why don't you come up to the office?"

'David and I went to see him, and he played us a song

that he liked and which he thought was just right for David. I didn't like it, but I thought that as he had had so many hits he was probably right – and David wanted a hit and he also relied on Macaulay's judgement then, whereas now he is much more dependent on his own judgement on every aspect and every detail of his career . . . the song was *Just For Tonight*, which we recorded for Macaulay and which was released on Pye . . . Macaulay spent £1,000 making that record, and he kept on changing it – but the record just did not happen, although David did get a TV out of it . . . looking back now, I think the explanation is that it just wasn't one of Tony's best songs.'

(Later David was to tell me himself that he made one mistake around this time – he turned down another of Tony Macaulay's songs *Build Me Up Buttercup* because he thought a number with a title like that could never be a hit. Instead, it was recorded by the Foundations, giving them a Number One hit in Britain and grossing over a million copies in world-wide sales.)

David Essex recorded just that one single for Pye before making another change of direction in his career – playing the Sultan Zelim in a Christmas show called *The Magic Carpet* which was presented at the Yvonne Arnaud Theatre, Guildford, towards the end of 1968. The script was written by actor John Dalby who also appeared in the production which had Alexander Donè as its director.

'David appeared in a white silk costume complete with turban, and there is still a portrait of him in the foyer of the theatre – looking much fuller in the face than he does now, because he weighed about a stone more in those days,' says Bowman. 'When they were in rehearsals Laurie

Lister told him: "Now, David – you are playing a Sultan Prince. My company of actors have very good speaking voices. You must not let us down. You really will have to work on your voice because you must sound more aristocratic than they do." And he really did work at it. By the time the show opened, his voice had changed – it was not a Cockney voice and yet it was not in the least aristocratic. But it worked.'

On the opening night, David received a telegram wishing him good luck from Susan Hampshire (who still followed everything he did) and her then husband Pierre Garnier-Deferre, and he received reviews in professionally more important papers than he had in the past.

In *The Financial Times*, which is noted for the quality of its coverage of the Arts and Entertainment, B. A. Young wrote:

> 'David Essex is one of the most promising recruits from the pop world I have seen for some time. He has the appealing immaturity which we like in pop singers but is capable of giving a perfectly adequate acting performance as well; his voice can fill the theatre without amplification of electronic equipment. Very nice looking, too. Watch this one.'

And the reviewer in *The Stage*, the leading weekly read by members of the acting profession, said:

> 'Handsome David Essex is excellent as the young Sultan. It is refreshing to find a male lead in a pantomime who can really sing.'

The show also produced David's very first fan letter –

from Anette Cliffe of The Clock Folly, Ashford Road, Laleham, Middlesex, who wrote:

> 'Dear David Essex,
> The pantermime of Araibian nights was very good. Everybody said you were very nice and I do, too, people say you are hansom to, every girl said that is included me. Love one of the girls at the pantermime, Anette Cliffe.'

Frank Dunlop, who later became a director at the National Theatre, saw David in the production at Guildford, and was so impressed that he suggested Derek Bowman contact the American director Donald Driver, who was casting replacements for the stage musical *Your Own Thing* – actors and actresses who would be ready to step into the leading roles for the remainder of the run when the originally contracted artistes left on the expiry of their contracts.

'The show was being presented at the Comedy Theatre by H. M. Tennent, and David was all set to step in after the first twelve weeks – but the show closed after ten weeks, which was a great disappointment for him,' says Bowman. 'As he had so often in the past, David now thought he was on the brink of a big break-through . . . and then it all slipped through his fingers through no fault of his own.'

Looking back, one cannot fail but to be impressed by the way in which both Bowman and David Essex kept going year in, year out, surmounting one setback after another; now, there was a third person in the picture, someone else to encourage David – Maureen Neal. She had been his girlfriend for several years since they had first met one night in an East End pub.

David had had a few drinks too many. In fact, he was – in his own words – paralytically drunk. He can remember going up to this very attractive girl at the bar, offering her a drink, and can remember very little after that. In fact, she bundled him into a taxi and saw him home – and when he woke up next morning he found a piece of paper in his pocket with her name and address on it. David phoned to apologise for being drunk the night before, and asked her out again – and they remained together after that, eventually marrying three or four years later at the registry office in Ilford with Derek Bowman as best man.

'We were all very amused by the officiating clerk,' says Bowman. 'It was just his manner. It is not something you could put on paper. It was very sad and poignant, really.'

And, as always, David Essex felt sure that his next record would be the one that gave him his break-through. By now he had left Pye, and had turned to his fourth recording company in five years – Decca – making the actual records with the freelance team of Chris Arnold, David Martin and Geoff Morrow, who were themselves successful songwriters who had written for Elvis Presley, had recorded their own material as Butterscotch, and also made a very good living advertising jingles for television. 'They raved about him,' says Bowman, 'but this was happening at a very bad time for us . . . just before David signed with them, I suffered a grievous blow. Over the space of four months, I lost both my mother and my father, and for a time I just didn't see how I could carry on. It was a real body blow . . . and in career terms for David, a hiatus. I told David that I thought that if he was going to become successful over the next few years, then he ought to find himself another manager . . . but David said: "No. I don't want to." He took the view that we had been through so much together that we could survive this, even though my mother had been such an inspiration to me . . . she was a remarkable woman. Her name was Bessie and my father's name was Joseph. She always wore velvet, and she was very musical. She inspired me in many ways – and later David dedicated one of the tracks on his album *Rock On* to her. It was "On and On." '

With the team of Arnold, Martin and Morrow, David Essex recorded his eighth British single, *That Takes Me Back/Lost Without Linda*. This was released by Decca on June 6th, 1969, the 25th anniversary of D-Day – and to commemorate this Decca distributed 500 toy landing craft to record reviewers and disc jockeys all over Britain, and with that the following biography of David, which reveals some facts to his career, even if it does get his age wrong: –

> 'Not many of today's pop singers can boast of a successful Royal Court audition. But then David Essex is not just a pop singer.
>
> 'Born in the East End of London 21 years ago, his father a docker and his mother a gypsy, David's first ambition was to be a professional footballer. In fact when he was 13 he played for the West Ham boys' Junior League.
>
> 'No-one can really predict which way a young boy's life will go and certainly no-one would have

thought that one rainy afternoon would completely change the course of David's. But with nothing to do he wandered around window shopping and came across a second-hand shop. In its window was a snare drum. David bought it and from then on all thoughts of a football career went from his mind.

'At the club where he was a member – a Dockland Settlement boys' club – he practised with his drum with encouragement from Sid Lipton's drummer. It was soon apparent that David had a natural aptitude and feel for music and it wasn't long before this musical interest took him to the West End clubs.

'His earliest recollection of clubs was when he was fourteen. With a friend he went down to the Flamingo and was caught by the atmosphere and live music. From then he made a weekly visit to the clubs and tucked himself in a corner and studied drummers' technique.

'When he was fifteen he decided it was time to join a band but his age was against him. But, undaunted, he said he was seventeen and he was accepted into the strict tempo world of a dance band.

'David recalls that five months of waltzes and foxtrots every night almost drove him scatty. Although realizing how invaluable the experience was he stuck it until he joined an amateur group called the China Plates Blues Band.

'Soon the group turned pro and in the next three years worked hard – including six months in Italy on the Adriatic and six months in the South of France.

'After six months in France the group returned to England and David decided it was time to leave. He was building a reputation more as a singer than a drummer and wanted to try the solo scene.

'It was at this time that he met his manager – showbiz writer Derek Bowman. Derek believed in David's talent and soon persuaded record companies of his potential. In the next three years David made six records but although they were all records to be proud of, they were the wrongs songs for hit parade status – one was *Love Story* which many top singers recorded including Jack Jones and Alan Price.

'Unlike many of his contemporaries, David was not willing to sit back and wait for things to happen. So between the times of making records be became an actor.

'It started when he answered an ad. in *The Stage* for actors wanted by a repertory company. He auditioned, passed, and for eight months toured with Zack Matalon's company to Salford, Henley, Norwich, etc.

'He then went on to play the lead in *The Fantastics*; the lisping Duke of Durham in the George and Ira Gershwin/P. G. Wodehouse musical *Oh! Kay!* and the lead in *Magic Carpet* at the Yvonne Arnaud Theatre, Guildford. During this period he was also trained by US negro coach Buddy Bradley in tap dancing and modern jazz dancing.

'One of David's big disappointments was when, because of his performance in *The Magic Carpet*, he was picked to take over the lead in the West End production of the American rock musical *Your Own Thing*, then before his debut the show closed.

'We now come back to the Royal Court audition. David read from Harold Pinter's *Caretaker* and from parts he'd already played and, as you know, it was successful.

'David has now been back in the recording studio – this time with Decca – with *That Takes Me Back*, an Arnold/Martin/Morrow compositions; produced by the composers, it's a soulful ballad from a writing team which is enjoying the distinction of having four songs on a new Elvis Presley album.

'It looks very much as though this is the song he's been waiting for and acting will have to take a back seat for a while.'

LIFELINES

STAGE NAME	David Essex
REAL NAME	David Cook
BIRTHDATE	July 23rd, 1947
BIRTHPLACE	Plaistow, East London
HEIGHT/WEIGHT	5ft. 10ins/11st.
EYES/HAIR	Blue/Black
PRESENT HOME	London and Romford
INSTRUMENTS PLAYED	Drums and piano
AGE ENTERED SHOW BIZ	18
FIRST IMPORTANT PUBLIC APPEARANCE	The Marquee
TV DEBUT	*Time for Blackburn*
RADIO DEBUT	*Radio One Club*

COMPOSITIONS	None
HOBBIES	Reading
FAVOURITE SINGERS	Melanie and Buddy Guy
FAVOURITE FOOD	Sausages
FAVOURITE DRINK	Whisky and Coke
FAVOURITE CLOTHES	Casual
MISCELLANEOUS LIKES	Nice people; country air
MISCELLANEOUS DISLIKES	Arrogance
TASTES IN MUSIC	Acid rock; classics; blues
PERSONAL AMBITION	To be happy and to find myself
PROFESSIONAL AMBITION	To play the lead at the National Theatre

But for all that, the single was unsuccessful – and so was the second one that David recorded on the Decca label, *The Day The Earth Stood Still/Is It So Strange?* which was released on September 26th, 1969. 'That was a monumental number, a real stormer,' says Bowman. 'But it sounded much too much like Barry Ryan, and did not get the airplay it needed ... we recorded a few other songs with Decca which were not released, and then we asked them to release us from the contract and returned to Arnold/Martin/Morrow, who were also recording a young negro singer from Detroit, Rozaa Wortham, who had a really beautiful voice and they suggested that she and David should record together as duo, which they did ... David's voice was too much under Rozaa's in the mixes. Meantime David's voice was beginning to develop very dramatically.

CHAPTER SIX

After Leslie Grade's illness, much of his work as a theatrical agent was taken over by his son, Michael, who approached Derek Bowman in the autumn of 1969 and asked whether David would like to work at the London Palladium – as understudy to Tommy Steele in that year's Christmas pantomime, *Dick Whittington*.

'My first reaction was to ask him why they couldn't find David a real job of his own instead of asking him to understudy someone else's, but it was good money and they were very good agents – and we thought it might lead to something else,' says Bowman. 'At the least, we thought David might get the opportunity to go on stage for a few nights, which is every understudy's dream . . . but Tommy seemed to have an iron constitution, and for two and half months David sat backstage at the Palladium sharing a dressing room with another understudy, who was doubling as a pantomime bear.'

Then on March 9th, 1970, a message came through to the theatre that Tommy had a sore throat and would not be able to get in for the matinee – and David was given just twenty minutes' warning that he would have to go on stage playing opposite Mary Hopkin as Alice Fitzwarren, and that he would have to sing a duet with her as well as singing one of Tommy's most famous numbers *Flash, Bang, Wallop*, which was a production routine originally featured in the London and Broadway stage success *Half A Sixpence*.

'You'll just have to do the best you can,' said the stage manager, aware that David was more than a little nervous. 'I was there – and I was more nervous than he was,' says Bowman, 'because no-one in the audience knew he was going on in Tommy's place . . . well, he got a big round of applause at the end of the show – and no-one asked for their money back.'

Less than two weeks later, on March 21st, David had another opportunity to play Dick Whittington – this time at both the matinee and evening performances, and with sufficient notice for him to be able to invite his mother and father, his wife, Derek and Derek's cousin, the actor Ron Moody, up to the theatre for the show. Also in the audience was the American film star Shirley Maclaine, Una Stubbs and Nicky Henson.

That night, he scored a great success with the *Flash, Bang, Wallop* routine and had to sing an encore – and at the end of the show Mary Hopkin and Kenneth Connor led him to the front of the stage to make a special bow, and to give a short curtain speech. Later, David received seventy fan letters from members of the audience.

'I was a little nervous at first,' David admitted afterwards, 'but the cast were marvellous to me and once I was on stage I felt fine. I really enjoyed it. To be honest, Tommy is so fit that I didn't think I would ever get a chance to appear . . . I was sitting backstage all that time for twelve weeks, through 120 performances, playing cards, watching TV and reading, never thinking my chance would come . . . I even started doing karate lessons at a place over the road.'

By now, more and more people were recognising the breadth of his talent. The disc jockey Alan Freeman described him as 'the guy who plugs on, a superstar for the top. He'll get through.' In the weekly pop music paper *The New Musical Express*, he was described as 'one of Britain's most under-rated singers'. The disc jockey and record company executive Jonathan King said he was 'very good' – just as Susan Hampshire, Peter O'Toole, Keith Michell, Zack Matalon, Ann Todd had all said over the years.

'I don't think my parents really accepted that this was my career until they saw me that night at the Palladium,' says David. 'Until then, I think my father had always had some doubts.' And Tommy Steele paid him the highest tribute one professional can pay to another when he returned to the Palladium on March 22nd, and walked into his dressing room to say: 'I've had to come back – I heard you were too bloody good, mate!'

By now, David and Maureen had moved to their first house – a small Victorian house in Seven Kings in the East End of London, which they had bought for £4,000 with a little financial help from both parents. When not at the Palladium, David decorated it – restoring all the original fireplaces and ceiling fittings, and adding to the Victorian atmosphere with wallpaper and other decorations from Biba's and other London stores.

What he really needed now, and this he realised himself, was the big break. He had spent six years preparing himself for it, acquiring far broader experience than many other artistes of his generation. I interviewed him around this time in a cafe just across the road from the Palladium, where he was on call at a few moments' notice, and he commented that the best advice he had ever had was something he had read in a magazine interview: 'It was something that Frank Sinatra said – that the breaks always come, but you have to be ready for them. The breaks always do come. I know there will be many more for me, and when the big one comes I'll be ready for it – because I've spent years learning to act, learning to dance, and learning how to sing on stage and handle an audience. I'm ready for the breaks . . . a Number One record means nothing these days because the important thing is being able to perform on stage. So many people get their big hits and then disappear because they were never prepared for the break, and it goes to their heads – it's still the same Sinatra thing, really.'

The remarkable thing about that quote is not its truth or its maturity but that it was said by someone who had still not had that big break, and was to go through another eighteen months of worse disappointments than he had ever known, before that break finally came. Of course, the hurdles were unknown and he had no idea what lay at the end of all that – which makes the perseverance of David Essex even more remarkable.

After the London Palladium pantomime, David was offered a part in the revue *Ten Years Hard* at the Mayfair Theatre, London, in which he appeared with Michael Flanders and Sally Smith, playing several parts – a hippie, an auctioneer, a policeman and a red-nosed comic. He also recorded those two singles with Rozaa Wortham, for which they called themselves David and Rozaa. The first was *Time Of Our Life/We Can Reach An Understanding* and this was released on September 4th, 1970, and then on March 13th, 1971, they had their second record issued, *The Spark That Lights The Flame/Two Can Share*. Both were on the Philips label.

'They were both produced by the Arnold/Martin/Morrow team, and Rozaa was a very fine singer,' says Bowman. 'David had met her in a London club. She used to go out with Muhammad Ali, and back home in Detroit she had entered a local heat and had then finally won the nationwide Miss Talent Contest that was organised in the United States by Pepsi Cola ... the first prize was 1,500 US dollars and she had also picked up twenty other trophies in the States, had worked with Jazz Workshop and with the New Christy Minstrels ... she sang in Spanish and German, and had sung in the film *Les Garçons Et Les Filles* ... we really had quite high hopes of those records.'

When the first one was released, the British music paper *Melody Maker* said this was 'definitely a hit' while in the rival *Record Mirror* Peter Jones said 'it is my personal pick of the week'. But, sadly, it proved to be David's tenth flop.

Meanwhile, David was going along to all the likely auditions – and landed small parts in the films *Carry On Henry*, *Assault* (which starred Suzy Kendall and Frank Finlay), and *All Coppers Are*. He also auditioned for *Vampire Circus*, a Hammer horror film! 'It's as well I didn't get it – or I would probably have ended up as a bat,' he said afterwards.

He had also been offered a role in another major pantomime, probably the leading one staged outside London – the Manchester production of *Cinderella* which opened on December 17th, 1970, with David playing Dandini, and again starring Mary Hopkin, only this time as Cinderella, with Lonnie Donegan as Buttons.

But apart from this pantomime and the release of the two David and Rozaa records and the occasional day of two's work as a film extra, his working life was very bleak – and in order to keep enough money coming in to pay his mortgage and the other regular bills, David took any job he could get. He cleaned windows, washed factory walls, drove lorries and delivered carpets.

'We were reaching a stage where every door seemed to be closing,' says Bowman. 'David had now released eleven records. None of them had been successful – and people just didn't want to know anything more about him. He was being written off, and it was a very depressing period . . . and it was at this time that he got the biggest disappointment of his whole career. He had been along to Ken Russell's office and auditioned for a part in the film musical version of *The Boy Friend*, which was being used as the vehicle to launch Twiggy into films, and he thought he had the main male lead in the film.

'We were both very excited because we realised this could be just the break he was waiting for . . . and for five weeks he rehearsed every day with Twiggy, becoming very friendly with her and with Justin de Villeneuve, who sold him his motorbike . . . after all those rehearsals I was beginning to feel that everything would be all right for him at last, which was a relief because I had been very worried for him with all these turn-downs from the record companies . . . everyone was very friendly down at the rehearsal rooms – and his friendship with Twiggy is one that lasts to this day . . . but just as they were getting ready to move into the studio, Ken Russell decided he didn't want David for the part – and he chose Christopher Gable instead . . . Twiggy fought for David, but it was no good – Russell was adamant, and Gable got the part . . . I have never known David so depressed as he was after that rejection. It was the low point of his whole career.

In the past, when the outlook was grim, David's wife Maureen had always gone out to work so that they had some money coming in each week. She had worked in an optician's shop and also in a boutique. But now she was pregnant.

'It was a terrible period for him,' says Bowman. 'His whole career seemed to come to a standstill. We were beginning to feel that no-one would ever want to offer him a recording contract again . . . he had felt quite humiliated in losing that part in *The Boy Friend*, and all he had now was the occasional day's work as a film extra.'

Although it was against his principles because he had always preferred to take any job, even window cleaning, rather than draw unemployment pay, David signed on at the local Labour Exchange. For nearly four months, he drew a weekly £5. 'The good thing about it was that they did pay your National Insurance stamp,' he told me soon afterwards, 'and so you don't suddenly find yourself faced with the problem of finding £75 to pay a year's stamps . . . The thing I didn't like was having to go down there each week in person to collect the money, standing in a queue in this Government building, painted like all Government buildings, green and cream, and so many of the people waiting in the queue with me had that beaten, knocked-about look.

'It was an unbelievable experience, and something I would hate to ever have to go through again. One day there was this one bloke standing in front of me who had obviously had a hard life that had left him with an unnatural respect for anyone who worked in an office. When it was his turn to go up to the counter, he doffed his cap and held it in his hand, and I heard him say: "It's 'ell for me bein' out of work – it's 'orror!" It was so pathetic seeing him standing there like that because you could see that he really wanted to work.

'So many of these poor people absolutely depend on the civil servants and their dole, and they treat them as though they're God . . . that poor chap who doffed his cap was given a ticket to be a liftman in an office block, so I suppose he'll spend the rest of his life going up and down a lift shaft for just a few pounds a week.'

This period out of work was totally demoralising. David told his father that he was thinking of giving up all hope of making a successful career in Entertainment, and his father phoned Bowman, who said: 'On no account must you encourage him to do that. He must not give up now.' David later told Bowman that he was thinking of leaving London and taking a job on a farm so that he could make a complete break with the past eight years. Between them, David's father and Derek Bowman talked him out of it. 'But make no mistake – this was the nadir of his life,' says Bowman.

And then Derek Bowman heard that H. M. Tennent was

planning to present a London stage production of *Godspell*, a musical that had originated in the States, was based on the Gospel of St. Matthew, and was widely seen as a rival to the immensely successful *Jesus Christ, Superstar*, which had not yet been staged in London despite its critical acclaim and box office success in America.

Even before the casting began, Bowman learned that H. M. Tennent would be presenting the show – and it just so happened that it had been this same company that had had David lined up earlier for the rock musical *Your Own Thing*, which had folded after ten weeks. 'I phoned Tony Howell, who was Binkie Beaumont's personal assistant, and asked him about this new show they were presenting . . . and then reminded him how much they had liked David when they wanted him to appear in *Your Own Thing* . . . he said they would like David to audition for a part, and asked whether he would like to go along the following week . . . by then, they thought Murray Head was going to play the part of Jesus Christ, but there was also the part of John the Baptist which had not yet been filled . . . apparently, they were thinking of Murray Head because he had sung the part of Jesus on the original LP version of *Jesus Christ, Superstar*, but in the end he dropped out of the part . . . but when David went along for the audition we didn't know that.'

Before the audition, David told Bowman bluntly that if he didn't get the part he would be quitting the business – and, of course, now we will never know whether he would have kept that promise or not. Certainly, he had now been completely out of work for nearly five months, had been drawing unemployment pay all that time, had found the process deeply humiliating, and with Maureen expecting the baby, was thinking he would have to find some other way of supporting her and the child.

Altogether, the producers of the show had considered around two thousand available actors for the various parts in *Godspell*. By the time, David went out on stage, the producers – Stuart Duncan, Joe Beruh and Edgar Lansbury (brother of Angela Lansbury) – were beginning to feel tired of all this constant auditioning of unknowns, and so was the director John Michael Tebelak and the musical director Stephen Schwartz.

They had all come over to London from the United States to recruit an all-British cast for the stage version to be presented in London, and on the way down to the Globe Theatre where the auditions were held, Bowman said to David Essex: 'You should sing *What A Mouth* or *Flash, Bang Wallop* – one of those numbers you understudied for Tommy Steele at the Palladium. That will make those Americans laugh.'

So David did, and after all those hours of routine auditions the producers did laugh. 'They fell about in the stalls,' says Bowman. 'And David sang it so well. I had always thought he was better than Tommy Steele himself with those numbers . . . he had rehearsed them so often that he had the characterisation, the movements and the lyrics just right . . . afterwards, the producers cut the numbers they had auditioned down to a short-list of twenty, including David, and he stood on one side of the stage with nine other people – and Murray Head was on the other side of the stage . . . the choice was between Murray Head and David, and then it emerged that Murray Head had another working commitment that would prevent him signing a long-term contract — but they knew that. David didn't.'

Suddenly John Michael Tebelak said: 'I would like you to play Jesus Christ.'

David did not know who he was talking to, and then turned round and looked over his shoulder before realising that it was he who had won the part.

'Would you like me to grow a beard?' asked David.

'No,' said Tebelak. 'It's not that kind of play. Our Jesus will have a red nose like a clown!'

CHAPTER SEVEN

When David Essex left the Globe Theatre to return home to his wife, Bowman says he seemed to have gone into a trance. 'He walked out of the room looking very distant and far-away,' says Bowman. When Maureen saw him, she thought something awful had happened. He was white-faced and unsmiling, and she knew what a strain he had been under. 'What's the matter?' she asked, and David replied: 'I'm Jesus!' And this he truly was – Jesus portrayed as a red-nosed harlequin clown with a tear on one cheek, a heart on his forehead, a Superman T-shirt, striped pants with big braces, and orange shoes with large pompons.

At the time, just after he had passed the auditions and before the show opened at the Roundhouse, David told me that he thought the essential difference of this Jesus compared with all the others that had been created in the theatre and on film was that 'he's played in the abstract, like an abstract painting. It depends on you as to what you see . . . Christ is played as a harlequin, and consequently he has pathos. There's no message in the musical at all other than the very fundamental one that we all have to co-exist with each other.'

For David Essex, this show was the turning point in his career; the moment at which he finally became a star after waiting eight years for the opportunity. For Derek Bowman, it was the moment of justification – the proof that 'my theories were right, that you could still establish yourself in the theatre and then move on to films without necessarily having to be in the hit parade.' But neither Essex nor Bowman nor even Binkie Beaumont of H. M. Tennent were really expecting *Godspell* to be as successful as it was. When the show was first assembled, it opened at the Roundhouse, a converted former British Railways engine shed in Camden Town to fairly mixed reviews, and it might easily have ended its run there – but the public turned up. Even there, it was a box office success – so H. M. Tennent transferred the production to Wyndham's Theatre in the Charing Cross Road.

'I think one of the most decisive factors was a review of the show when it was still being presented at the Round house that was written for *The Sunday Times* by Harold Hobson, who was the doyen of all the London theatre critics,' says Bowman. 'This review was the sort of review that a professional actor can wait for all his life . . . and Hobson not only reviewed the show once, but when it was transferred to Wyndham's he returned again and wrote another review, which was even better than the first . . . it was the sort of accolade that could be the crowning point to many an actor's career.'

The first review appeared in *The Sunday Times* on November 21st, 1971, when Harold Hobson wrote:

> 'There are many fine performances now to be seen in London but if I had to choose a single one to show to a visitor it would be this Christ, this simple wondering Christ played by David Essex. The shining thing about Mr. Essex's performance is its manifest,

stirring incapacity to perceive evil or to recognise mockery. It inhabits a world in which there is no guile and no cruelty. But it is not a simplicity to be made a fool of: it's meekness is as strong as it is true. Mr. Essex, and with him the whole company, rises to extreme heights in the scenes of the Last Supper and the Agony in the Garden.'

The second review appeared in *The Sunday Times* on February 27th, 1972, and this time Harold Hobson wrote:

'It is my firm opinion that Mr. Essex's is the best performance in London, the least histrionic, the happiest and the most moving. That it should be so at a time when we all marvel at Olivier's prestigious James Tyrone, one of the greatest actors' finest creations, is a measure of Mr. Essex's achievement.'

Those were the two reviews that made the impact within David Essex's profession; the reviews that made other actors and musicians want to see the show for themselves; that drew politicians, bishops and other celebrities to every performance – that made David Essex himself a star, much sought after for films, for other stage productions, for TV appearances, and that re-opened the doors to the recording companies. There were other reviews, too:

'The show is not irreverent, neither is it against Christ – it is very much with him. But it tries to strip away the glitter from religion and shows Jesus as I believe he was – a revolutionary and a prophet, but also a real person . . . a boyish clown hero in beach pants and red nose who holds his followers together with non-stop games.'

– The Times

'As a youthful boyish Christ, David Essex is appropriately gentle and modest. However he is given nothing to do which provides the slightest hint of what Jesus was about. His death is particularly unmoving and anti-climatic.'

– The Evening Standard

'A jumping, jolly, happy, hippie musical with a robust, rocking beat. Jesus is played by a young Londoner David Essex in a Superman sweatshirt and clown's make-up and a fine job he makes of it.'

– The Sunday Mirror

'A GREAT ADVERT FOR GOD'
– headline in Melody Maker

'One must mention David Essex who plays Jesus because in a very difficult part which might easily have lapsed into bad taste or have given offence, he never put a foot wrong.'

– The Catholic Herald

'David Essex, having done all manner of things with a marked lack of success, can be said to have arrived at last, courtesy of that most famous trouper of all time, Jesus Christ.'

– Disc and Music Echo

With such acclaim, the show quickly became one of the most successful in London with the rich, the famous and the successful anxious to see it. Cliff Richard went backstage after one performance and told David that he thought the show was 'fantastic, marvellous, one of the best shows I have ever seen'. Other visitors included Noel Coward, Claudette Colbert, Lord Longford, Spike Milligan (who wrote David a personal letter of congratulation afterwards), Peter Sellers, the Dean of Johannesburg, Paul and Linda McCartney, Georgie Fame, Pete and Karen Townshend, Prince Charles, Princess Anne, George and Patti Harrison, Ingrid Bergman, Bishop John Robinson, the Bishop of Coventry, Judi Dench, Dame Sybil Thorndike, Ann Todd, Susan Hampshire (of course), Alec McCowan.

Rab Butler, the former Conservative Foreign Secretary and Chancellor of the Exchequer and now Master of Trinity College, Cambridge, wrote:

> 'I would like you to know how much my wife and I and a party enjoyed your *Godspell*. You seemed, if I may say so, to combine reverence with gaiety and to make the story of St. Matthew, which has interested the world for so many years, into something living in modern times.'

The distinguished actor Tony Britton wrote from the Vaudeville Theatre, asking for David's autograph for 'my daughter Fern – she thinks you're out of sight, and I thought you were absolutely splendid'. The distinguished film producer Bryan Forbes brought his daughter Sarah to

2. David as he appeared in *Godspell*.

3. Recording *Lamp Light*.

4. David with his Gold Disc for *Rock On*.

5. Disc awards 1974. David Essex and Lynsey de Paul photographed after receiving their awards.

6. David autographing albums.

7. A still from *Stardust*.

8. Two pictures of David from *That'll be the Day*.

10. David relaxing in the recording studio.

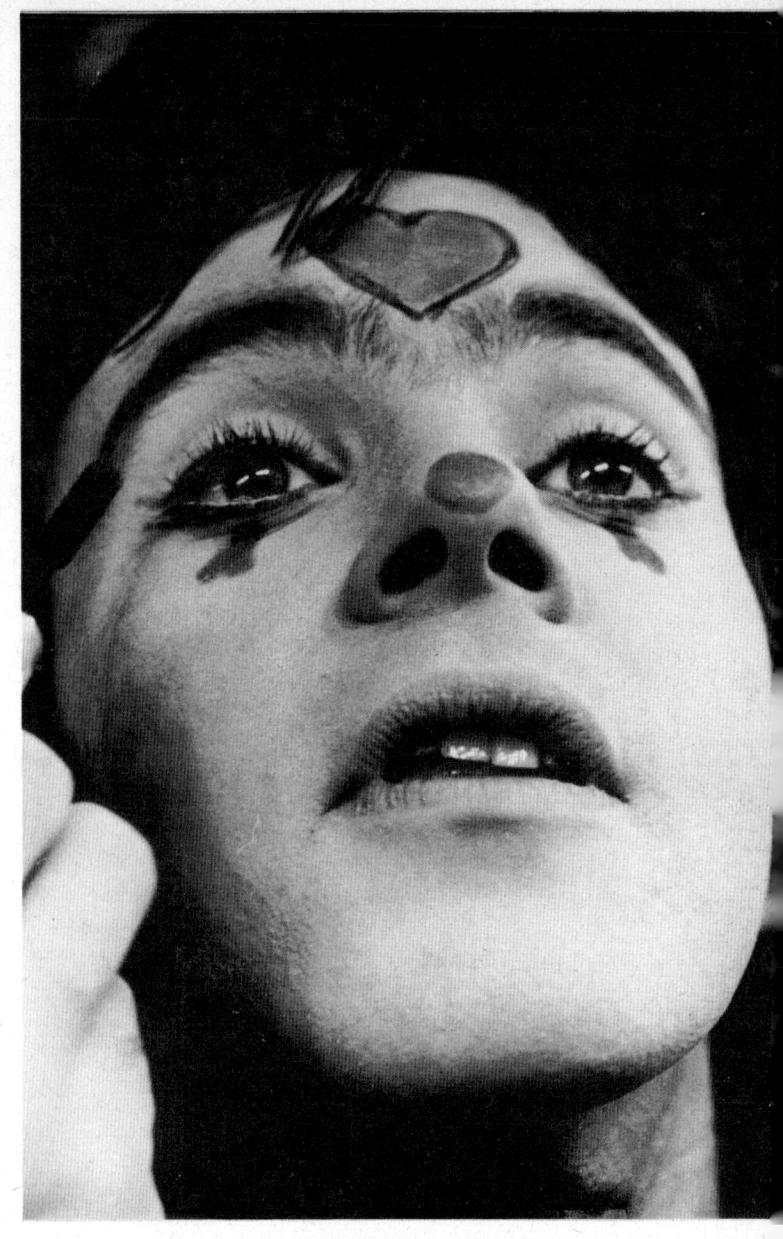

11. Making up for *Godspell*.

12. Riding is one of David's hobbies.

14. David Essex and Marsha Hunt.

15. A still from *Stardust*. On the drums is Keith Moon, on the guitar, Dave Edmunds in the group Stray Cats.

16. David is pictured here with 'Ditto' Drummer Keith Moon (second

17. A still from the film *That'll be the Day*.

18. David posing outside Wyndham's Theatre during the *Godspell* run.

19. David clowns.

20. David photographed during the shooting of his new film *Stardust*.

21. David pictured as the lead singer in the Stray Cats pop group during *Stardust*, 1974.

22. The most recent picture of David Essex.

the theatre as the one special treat she wanted on her thirteenth birthday. After one performance, the head of the Church of England himself, the Archbishop of Canterbury, Dr. Michael Ramsay, went backstage and said: 'I loved it ... you have given me such a big blessing, and I can only give you such a small one back.' And then he blessed David in his dressing room.

And it wasn't just a steady succession of famous people who came to see him. Soon, he was getting sacks of fanmail at the theatre – and girls were knitting him scarves and sweaters, and socks, and writing poems, and painting his portrait. Thirty girls at a school in Kingston-upon-Thames, Surrey, each wrote him a poem and sent it to him on a decorated scroll that arrived in a protective cardboard tube. 'That worried me at first,' said David. 'When I saw this big parcel, I thought it might be a bomb from the IRA.'

I used to see him regularly at the theatre or at a wine bar nearby, and the remarkable thing about his success was that he could walk down any London street – recognised but unmolested. Every day he would either ride up to town in his five year old Mercedes car, which he had nicknamed Cronk, or the red Triumph motorbike that he had brought from Justin de Villeneuve, usually wearing the denim dungarees which he used to buy from the Army and Navy Stores because they were cheap and hard-wearing. Across the walls of his large, tall dressing room were telegrams and personal letters from people who had seen him in the show; drawings from fans; furry gonks – and a poster proclaiming THIS IS JERUSALEM CITY OF PEACE. But he was careful not to be over-identified with the various religious organisations that were anxious to recruit him.

'I've never been particularly religious,' he told me one day, 'and now I'm always getting invited to preach sermons, which seems very strange to me because I'm an actor not a clergyman. I don't do any of that. I don't want to get too involved in the religious side of it, but I don't mind going to charity functions. I'm always getting invited to those, too – and I always go if I can, as long as it's a cause that I agree with.'

Among those he did help were the Variety Club of Great Britain, the Stars Organisation for Spastics, the Sunshine Fund for Blind Babies, a housing society for rasing funds for elderly Jewish ex-servicemen and for crippled children.

Sometimes, the requests and the gifts that he received surprised him. One day he opened a parcel – and found a pair of underpants. Another time, he unwrapped a seventeen-jewel wrist watch. And he received many presentation sets of Parker and Sheaffer pens. In one of our interviews, he had told me that because of his gypsy background on his mother's side he was superstitious about black cats – and also about the colours mauve and yellow in any combination.

'I should never have told you that,' he said, after the magazine article appeared. 'Ever since then I've been receiving paintings, drawings and presents wrapped in mauve and yellow ribbons. One girl sent me a wine bottle converted into an ornament with mauve and yellow candle wax . . . another day I opened a parcel and found a 15ft long scarf, knitted in mauve and yellow wool . . . and I keep getting gonks, toy cats and dogs, socks and pullovers knitted in mauve and yellow.'

By now he had moved from the Victorian house in Seven Kings to a modern town house, with a study of his own – and three steel filing cabinets into which he packed every fan letter he received. 'I've never thrown one away,' he told me. 'If someone threw away a letter that I had written, I would be offended . . . so naturally I've kept all the letters that have been sent to me,' he said.

If he found his sudden elevation to the ranks of the teenybop idols surprising, it did not unnerve him; in some interviews he started to talk more seriously about the role he was playing.

He told the magazine *Petticoat* that he saw Jesus as a humble, real man who laughed and cried, without any kind of glitter around him. 'You can dismiss the Jesus thing as being "in", but the younger generation have discovered the man who makes the most sense, that the best philosopher and teacher is Jesus,' he said. 'They've gone through a search for the complete mystic experience without too much success; they've tried drugs, they've tried Eastern religions and lots of them found it didn't work. Jesus has got a terribly romantic image. He was the Che Guevara of that time, the underdog in an occupied country. They identify with Him as a revolutionary with a revolutionary band of disciples. I don't know if the kids identify with the half divine, half-man image, but as far as Jesus as a kind of man goes he tends to be appealing . . . I get letters every day from kids who say that for the first time they can see what Jesus was, they can see him as a real person with a sense of humour.'

Then he told *Record Mirror* that 'religion wasn't relevant all of a sudden, but the way we present it with a sense of humour, and the way we illustrate the parables, it probably makes it seem more relevant again. It's a valid piece of theatre as much as a play by Harold Pinter would be, but with all the press we had before the opening and the outrageous sound of the idea some people were going bananas about it.'

But in less serious moments, he would remind journalists – as he frequently told me – that he was an actor, that he was a rock singer, that he would like to start recording his own material, that he would like to appear with his own backing band, that what he was thinking about now was his next role, his next record. 'I've had five or six films offered to me,' he told me one night, 'but I've turned them all down because they're not the sort of films I want to do . . . I don't want to do one of these films about the swinging London set because that never really existed other than in the minds of the press.' Later, he was to reveal that he had also turned down the opportunity to make a TV series with Lulu. 'Isn't that strange,' he commented. 'Years ago I would have jumped at a chance like that – now I'm getting offers from all directions; the recording companies are competing against each other to try and get me to sign for them.'

With some of the other artistes appearing in *Godspell*, he briefly formed his own group – with Julie Covington and Marti Webb, two of the girl singers, and with lead guitarist Lance Dowen, bass player Mike Thorne and drummer Tony Morton. 'We started doing shows on Sunday nights, which was our night off . . . but I had to finish that because I found I was so exhausted after a week in the theatre that I really needed the Sunday off to rest.'

One of those shows was at the Music Workshop, and David was a little embarrassed to find that Paul and Linda McCartney were in the audience – because his act included Paul's song *Maybe I'm Amazed* and two well-known Beatles numbers *Long Winding Road* and *She came In Through The Bathroom Window*. 'They were very nice, though,' David told me later. 'At the end of our act, Paul and Linda both rose to their feet and clapped, which I thought was very kind of them.' Later when David achieved recording fame Paul and Linda joined him in a chorus on his hit *Gonna Make You A Star* on 'Top of the Pops'.

But that was just a short-lived excursion – he was much more serious about working on a solo album with his friend record producer Jeff Wayne, who had previously worked as an arranger for the Righteous Brothers, whose single *You've Lost That Loving Feeling* had long been one of David's all-time favourites. But first there was the problem of an old contract from which Derek Bowman was negotiating a release, and there was the one film offer that really did interest him – the invitation to play the lead role of Jim Maclaine, the embryonic pop star, in the movie *That'll Be The Day*.

CHAPTER EIGHT

What appealed to David Essex about the role of Jim Maclaine in *That'll Be The Day* was that the character was one he could relate to, a boy from a working class background who had rejected the more conventional opportunities open to him and had drifted into pop music after working as a deck chair attendant, in a holiday camp, and on a fairground. This was an attitude of mind that David understood even though the film was set a few years earlier than his own life story was — it was closer in time to the first generation of British rock stars, the Beatles, the Rolling Stones, the Kinks, the Who, etc., than it was to David's.

'I was sent the script of *That'll Be The Day*, and I was very interested,' he told *Melody Maker*, 'but the producers didn't think I had the right nasty qualifications for the part. Playing Jesus wasn't really the right preparation for Jim Maclaine . . . but I told them I could be a bastard. I did the screen test and they seemed to like it, so I got the part. I didn't want to be stereotyped and I think the role shocked some people . . . when you get to a certain level of success in one particular area it seems to confuse a lot of people. They have a preconceived idea that I'm England's answer to David Cassidy or whatever. I'm not. That's why *That'll Be The Day* probably shocked a few people. There was Jesus with his dick hanging out.'

By now the music papers were starting to show interest

in David Essex, and he told *The New Musical Express* that he thought 'my era was important, but not as important as Maclaine's. By my time the working class kid had already gained some kind of respect in society. Now it's accepted that you can come from wherever and get somewhere if you push hard enough. Before, there wasn't anything unless you were academically very strong. You just did an apprenticeship or what your father did. You either had it or you didn't. The film is really an important social document as well as being a bit of entertainment.'

The other attraction was that he was at heart a rock 'n' roller from way back, tinged with rhythm 'n' blues. 'It's going to be a very nostalgic sort of film for me to do,' he told me just before he took seven weeks off from *Godspell* in the autumn of 1972 to go down to the Isle of Wight where he and Maureen and their baby daughter Verity Lee rented a cottage while the film was shot on location. We discussed the project before he went and afterwards.

The remarkable thing about the film, which subsequently became one of the major box office successes of 1973, was that the producer David Puttnam's Good Times Enterprises company made it within a 500,000 US dollar budget with a production schedule of just seven weeks. The idea had been in Puttman's mind for some years, and he told *Disc and Music Echo* that 'the reason *That'll Be The Day* never came out when I first thought of it was that nobody in the film industry would believe that anybody was remotely interested in what happened in the early fifties ... I started off as a bona fide film freak rather than a business man, and I couldn't take that disinterested attitude they have. The most ghastly experience I had was to spend a year on a film I hated. That was *The Pied Piper* starring Donovan and I just never felt right about it.'

'The producer and the director both came to see me in *Godspell* before offering me the part, and they already had Ringo lined up to play Mike, who was to be my best friend in the film . . . that was strange because up to that time I had never met him. One of the important scenes in the film was set in a ballroom where we were both jiving, and I had never jived before, either – so during the afternoons while I was still in *Godspell* I went along to the Dance Centre in Floral Street, Covent Garden, to learn to jive. I started meeting Ringo occasionally so that we could get to know each other before the film started, which was essential if he was to be my best friend – and I discovered that he was a good jiver, a pretty trendy jiver. Of course, that was all before my time.

'We had to meet because it's important to have a relationship with someone who is supposed to be your best friend . . . the other strange thing about it for me was that the film was set in the Provinces in the early fifties, strange because I had never lived outside London, and was still at primary school at the time, so I went down to the Raven public house in the East End, where the Teddy Boys still go every night as their pub, just to see how they stood and how they spoke so that I got the mannerisms right.'

Among the musicians who worked on the film's music at different stages were Pete Townshend of the Who, Keith Moon of the Who (who played the drummer J. D. Clover), Stevie Winwood and Jim Capaldi of Traffic, Graham Bond and, of course, Billy Fury, one of the most successful singers of the late fifties who appeard in gold lamé in a ballroom sequence.

'In the film, Jim Maclaine is on the verge of being a Teddy Boy,' David told me. 'I never was one, but I can remember seeing the Teds walking round the East End with their drapes and drainpipe trousers and brothel creeper shoes . . . I'd never even played a part like that before as an extra. In *Assault*, which starred Frank Finlay, I was just a young fellow . . . and in *All Coppers Are*, I was a boy in a boarding house that some gangsters had moved into . . . but I've always liked rock 'n' roll. It was a very important period in time because it was an advertisement for youth . . . for the first time young people were brought to the forefront . . . in the film, Maclaine is a boy who could have gone to University, but instead he turns to music . . . this character really does not know that he is one of the revolutionaries of the time, because this is set in the beginning , a sort of pre-war-Beatles, although it's not as simple as that . . . Ringo has had to have his hair cut short like a Teddy Boy, and as soon as I leave *Godspell* my own hair has got to be cut short to fifties length . . . it was all much more natural for Ringo because he lived through the whole period, and had just left school when it started, and, of course, he did work in a holiday camp himself when he was with Rory Storm and the Hurricanes before he joined the Beatles.

'The closest I came to that was buying my first records – the very first records I bought were *See You Later, Alligator* by Bill Haley and the Comets, and *Bony Marony* by Larry Williams, and I was very into Buddy Holly, who I always thought was fantastic, and Little Richard, too, though I was not so big on Eddie Cochran, who was another of the very big influences on the rock musicians growing up at that time ... Jim Maclaine grows up aware of all these records. He doesn't want to go to university, but he would have liked to go to art school if he could ... instead his mother finds him working on the deck chairs, and then he goes to the holiday camp and the funfair, working on the Whip, with Ringo as his bad influence ... all the time he's writing poetry, which will probably become songs eventually, and he's also playing the harmonica, and at the end of the film he starts to play guitar for the first time.

'The nearest I ever came to the stars of that time was when I was with the Everons, and we were booked to appear in a concert with Bill Haley and the Comets round about 1964 – when he was top of the bill. That was at Bishops Stortford ... and then I saw the Everly Brothers once when they were appearing at the London Palladium.

'At the time all that started, I was only seven or eight years old ... I started buying records and getting interested in fashion and styles about 1956, but I didn't get much money for that before I was about eleven years old when I was working in the Rathbone Street market in Canning Town on the fruit stall, and used to pick up about twenty five bob a week from that ... the big thing in the East End when I was going through secondary school was the Mods, who used to drive around on scooters in their little pink jeans ... I was like that with my little Italian suit with the bum freezer jacket, and I thought I looked really smart with my slim ties, my brogue shoes, Crombie overcoats and those little hats.

'Now I've got some clothes of that Teddy Boy period, too – when we finished the film they let me keep all the clothes that I had worn for the different scenes. Always in films, you have to have three sets of each costume – so that one can be cleaned and one kept spare for every scene. And so now I've got three Teddy Boy suits – and three pairs of blue suede shoes!'

Working on the film with Ringo, he formed a friendship with the former Beatle – though Ringo subsequently dropped out of the sequel, *Stardust*, explaining that 'having lived through the madness once, I couldn't experience it a second time. It's too close to home.' In *That'll Be The Day*, which took its title from the Buddy Holly hit from the late fifties, Ringo was the cynical older, more world-weary Ted who had seen it all. 'I wouldn't have played David's part in a million years,' he said, 'but I like my character because I really felt I could get hold of it, draw on myself, on people I knew and from the experience of living through that period.'

Certainly, David Essex himself felt that he had learned much – though he found it strange shooting a film in winter that was supposed to be set in the summer months after the school term had ended. 'Ringo and I were in T-shirts all the time pretending to be having a good time when all the time it was pouring rain,' he told me. 'We did a lot of night shooting for the funfair sequences, where Ringo and I are seen working the fair . . . that was great because we had the run of the funfair all night. I didn't find that too strange because years ago I used to work on a funfair, and I had to teach Ringo how to balance as we went round the rides collecting money from the punters . . . I told him the dodge that we used to get up to in my day which was to take someone's £1 note just as the ride was starting up, and then when the ride was over you'd deny that they'd ever given you the £1 – that was a standard dodge on the East End fairs.

'We had great fun travelling round on all the rides and the dodgems between takes – it was like being a kid all over again . . . and I got talking to Ringo about the past . . . he told me of the days when he used to be a barman on the Mersey Ferry, and showed me how to handle a tray of glasses and balance them over my head . . . one night at the hotel where the rest of the cast were staying, we started playing in the ballroom. There was Ringo on lead guitar, me on bass, Keith Moon on organ, Graham Bond on drums, Harry Nilsson on tambourine and Honky Tonk on saxophone . . . and we had Billy Fury as our singer . . . you never heard such a noise in your life because we were all playing about with instruments that we don't normally play just for the fun of it, and in the end the manager must have had enough – because the Police suddenly materialised around 4 a.m. in the morning and asked us to be quiet.

'You know how mad Keith Moon is. One day a helicopter suddenly arrived and landed on the lawn outside the hotel – and out stepped Moon. "It's the only way to travel, man!" he said . . . he'd decided not to come down by car and boat that day, and had ordered a helicopter to pick him up at his home in Chertsey.'

The result of spending seven weeks in close confinement with Ringo and Keith Moon, Billy Fury, Harry Nilsson, etc., was that David found himself accepted by a generation of artistes who had been successful for many years longer than he had – sometimes a difficult bridge to cross. Now, they all see each other socially – and among the ornaments at his recently bought 16th century home in Essex, David has two of Ringo's sculptures, one a milk bottle and the other a Coke bottle.

The success of the film lay partly in its nostalgia, partly in its music – and partly in the relationship that developed between these two on the screen; David the innocent and sexually inexperienced teenager who had no sense of direction, and Ringo the crudely cynical, yet strangely tender and understanding older friend giving Jim Maclaine almost brotherly guidance. But no-one, least of all David, expected the film to be the outstanding success that it was. It was released in April, 1973 – and became an immediate box office success, with the soundtrack album an equally fast best-seller. The critics liked David's performance, too:

> 'A study of adolescence at once honest and harsh, persuasive and sad, and sometimes very funny . . . Mr. Essex's charm as an actor renders this charmless character not only bearable, but interesting.'
> – Eric Shorter, *The Daily Telegraph*

> 'David Essex, making his lead debut in films, is excellent as the school-blazered boy from a home where Dad has already gone off on his own impatient feet, who makes a break on the eve of the big exam. Neither a rebel nor cause-seeker; just a drifter, really.'
> – Alexander Walker, *Evening Standard*

'A fascinating social document . . . the teenage yobo-hero, played by David Essex with just the right lazy-voiced cockiness.'
— Cecil Wilson, *The Daily Mail*

'David Essex does well at rounding out a character with a historical context.'
— David Robinson, *The Times*

'David Essex is the star and does a great job.'
— Kenneth Bailey, *Sunday People*

'Mr. Essex is a real find; a natural actor with an astonishing quality of stillness in him and an uncanny grasp (quite unusual in a first major performance) of just how much the camera needs from an actor more familiar with the techniques of the theatre.'
— David Castell, *Films Illustrated*

'Mr. Essex is excellently found as the rootless boy-man.'
— John Coleman, *New Statesman*

'David Essex . . . throwaway playing . . . remarkable development in proletarian playing in British cinema.'
— Dilys Powell, *The Sunday Times*

'Jim has all the ambivalence of the rebel hero . . . but retains his attraction (which is a measure of the force of Ray Connolly's script and David Essex's portrayal).'
— John Pidgeon, *New Musical Express*

'David Essex is excellent as the confused youth and this must certainly be his year in music and films.'
— Gavin Petrie, *Disc and Music Echo*

'The film is nicely acted with a particularly engaging performance from David Essex.'
— Sue Darcy, *Photoplay*

'David Essex in his first film is just right for Jim, understating the character, allowing enough room for easy identification and sympathy.'
— Celia Roberts, *What's On*

'David Essex is splendidly natural as the boy without stability or direction.'
— Molly Plowright, *Glasgow Herald*

'Set in the late fifties, it's an accurate picture of an A-level drop-out, Jim Maclaine, well played by newcomer David Essex.'
— Gavin Millar, *The Listener*

'With his supremely photogenic face and total plasticity of movement he would do well enough as a cipher without destroying the impact of the film one iota, but the fact that he is a considerable actor, one who can portray a diffident shiny-faced schoolboy at one moment and a seedily determined roué the next, is a subtle feat of the Jekyll and Hyde — made all the more astonishing by the fact that the transition has been performed almost without one noticing it. It will be interesting to see how this welcome and riveting debut will be followed.'

– Julian Fox, *Films and Filming*

With such excellent reviews and an acceptance by his peers David Essex now felt ready to return to his first love – rock music. The doors of the recording companies were now well and truly open, with executives almost falling over each other trying to secure his signature to a long-term contract. 'My producer is in a meeting with one record company,' David told *The New Musical Express*, 'and another company rings up – "Can I talk to you about David Essex?" – and he goes outside and it's an offer double what he's been talking about in the meeting. It's all gone bang! I'm amazed that I've been accepted on all the fronts I've attacked. Stage, film and the latest thing, the songs I've started writing. I still feel very much based in music and it would be lovely to actually finish the songs off, because I feel I was side-tracked off all that . . . I always thought other people knew better than I did because they had Rolls Royces, but they don't. That's why I left it. Now I've come back and it's started working.'

What had really happened, without this ever being the intention of David Essex or Derek Bowman, was that they had broken every rule of the rock 'n' roll game. They had come in at the top. And David Essex had become a rock 'n' roll star with his photo in every teenage magazine and on cinema posters all over the country without him ever having a hit record. Now he was ready to prove that he could do that, too.

CHAPTER NINE

While David Essex was working on *That'll Be The Day*, Pete Townshend of the Who wrote a number titled *Keep On Rocking* that was at one time all lined up to be David Essex's first single since his stage success in *Godspell*. David recorded the song and was quite keen to release it, but before that opportunity came – because by then Derek Bowman was now near to securing his release from that old contract – David wrote another song himself. He called it *Rock On*.

He actually wrote it on the film set itself. 'In between sitting around and eating nuts and waiting to be filmed,' he said in an interview with *The New Musical Express* discussing the way he and producer Jeff Wayne had made the record. 'Basically, we wanted a record that was kind of evil-but-funny. I like to put two things together and to have, like, perhaps a light lyric with heavy music or heavy lyric with light music. It takes the edge off it's being pretentious and heavy.' The song had a very nostalgic fifties feel with references to blue suede shoes, James Dean, etc. 'I think most people thought I'd do a quick Cassidy – like, a really successful eighteen months doing old ballads,' he said. But that he did not do.

Instead, *Rock On* was a rock 'n' roll record with a haunting use of reverb. As the American paper *The Village Voice* put it, 'instead of getting carried away with the cheap sentiments aspect of the echo chamber, Essex and producer Jeff Wayne carefully set up an infinite regress situation, placing the listener right in the middle of two sound mirrors set face-to-face. It's all coming right at you while it's all being spirited back into the sound oblivion from which it all came.'

Having heard the cut, CBS Records signed him to a five year contract with a large advance – and launched the record and David in a white silk suit at a press reception at Quaglino's in August, 1973, issuing photographs by David Bailey to the press complete with a kit containing a potted biography in question and answer form.

The record went to Number One in the British charts in September; became a hit throughout Europe – and went to Number One in the American charts in March, 1974, winning David a gold disc from the Recording Industry Association of America for 1,000,000 US dollar sales. Within six months, the single had sold over 2,000,000 copies around the world, and it is still selling.

Critically, its reception was mixed in the music papers who had been watching David Essex develop his career, with some scepticism.

> 'More than a pretty face, more than a slender waist, this man has the guts to put out a positively thirst-quenching hit 45 – a rumble of bass, a patter of bongoes, a voice laced in reverb, and a glance back to blue jeans, baby queen, James Dean and other desultory 50's people. A feast of subtleties: will mess with your mind.'
> – *The New Musical Express*

'By the Gods, this smells nay reeks of Beefheart. I mean, this isn't fair, we chaps up here at Batley Fiesta expected something, well . . . a little more conventional. No lush orchestration? No turgid strings? No bespectacled lady choruses and J. Arthur cymbal crashes? What happened to the descending scale tubular bell bit, then? Bopper schmopper. I think if young Donny heard this he would as they say tear his hair and rent his clothes, crying aloud "This is the work of Beelzebub", smiting the turntable with a fiery cross. A double-tracked warpy sounding bass takes you by the ear leading you through possibly the best and most suggestive single cut this year. David's voice is beautifully perverted through carefully applied echo, which seems to have been used on everything bar the strangely wilting, slicing strings that leap briefly across the horizon towards the middle . . . magnificent to be sure and written by David himself. Certainly not the polite schmaltz everyone would lead you to expect. It'll either be colossal or disappear without a trace.'
— *Disc and Music Echo*

'Interesting introduction creating a mood of harsh surrealism, a pastiche of the cosmic force, attacking one's lugholes with fierce discords and horrifying *Back Off Bugaloo* style riffing. At least that is the view of Horace Ruby our legitimate rock correspondent. My view? Absolute clap-trap.'
— *Melody Maker*

With a hit record and one of the most successful films of the year touring the country, David finally left *Godspell* on September 15th, 1973, and over the next five months before he started working on the follow-up to *That'll Be The Day*, he spent much of his time on promotion. In the October, he briefly visited Holland, France and Germany for TV appearances. Then in November he flew to the States to appear in person at special showings of the film in New York, Phoenix, Los Angeles, San Francisco, Seattle, Denver, Houston, Dallas, Fort Worth, Philadelphia and Boston, appearing on all the local TV and radio stations. 'I miss my wife,' he told *Rolling Stone*.

Soon the awards started to flow in. He won the Variety Club of Great Britain Award as the Most Promising Newcomer of 1973, which must have seemed strange after nine years in the business – and the *Disc and Music Echo* award as the Brightest Hope for 1974. He released two more singles *Lamplight* and *America* – and received one of the annual *New Musical Express* awards for *Rock On*, which was judged the Best British Produced Pop Record of 1973. CBS won the award for the Best British Marketing Concept.

By now he was being treated as a star. He had a big new country home and a new car. He was turning down many more offers than he accepted. And he was ready for the next two major developments in his career, *Stardust* – and tours with his own band. It had taken a long time. But he was ready.

CHAPTER TEN

Just as Derek Bowman always thought of David Essex as a star, so David himself has always behaved as though he was one – and on the set of *Stardust* the film's writer Ray Connolly commented: 'He moves and looks like a true star. He's perfect for the part. And therein, perhaps, lies the secret of the David Essex success story.'

He has that essential charismatic quality that makes the Superstar. No-one can define it because this comes in many forms – but you just have to see John Lennon or Paul McCartney walk into a room, Mick Jagger seize a mircophone on stage, Marlon Brando walk across a film set, Sammy Davis smile, Gary Glitter stride into a studio or Shirley Bassey extend her arms towards her audience and you know in that moment that they have something extra that words cannot convey. And David Essex has it.

It was something that I first became aware of when I interviewed him backstage at the London Palladium when he was Tommy Steele's understudy; he had much more confidence, a clearer sense of direction, than one usually sees in young artistes – and that strange blend of arrogance and humility that all the really successful have.

While I have been working on this book David has been finishing the production work on *Stardust* in Britain, Spain and the United States, and a recording schedule in France; for some months he has given few interviews; this third single *America* has been relatively unsuccessful in Britain, yet in Europe alone it has sold 350,000 copies. Essex had sold 3 million record units throughout the world by the early autumn of 1974 and I have no doubt at all that when the film is released, when he begins his live concert tours (which were pencilled into his diary for the autumn of 1974), David Essex will be acclaimed as the Superstar he is. All the signs are there.

Even before he stared making records again, David Essex was being inundated with fan mail and gifts while he was appearing at Wyndham's Theatre in *Godspell* – which is a rare response for a stage artist to receive. He can no longer walk down a London street unrecognised.

When members of his fan club were invited to a special show at Belle Vue, Manchester, in March to be filmed as a scene for *Stardust* there were riots in the audience – even though this was just a scene in the film. Afterwards, Keith Moon (who plays the drummer J. D. Clover in the film) said: 'I thought they'd have to be told when to scream and so on, but as it happened a kind of hysteria took hold and after a few seconds on stage all hell broke loose. Afterwards, the kids were asking where the group was playing next. They'd forgotten I was in *The Who*.'

Already, by refusing to talk too much about his private life, about his new home and his family, Essex has established a certain mystery about himself – and this will be emphasised by his role as Jim Maclaine in *Stardust* in which he plays a singer plucked from an obscure band who achieves international fame, and then retreats from it to a castle in Spain. 'It's a very powerful film,' Derek Bowman told me after they had finished filming but before the editing was complete. 'If it gets a double-A certificate, it will be lucky . . . because David filmed scenes in bed with two nude girls, and with himself very obviously naked beneath the sheets . . . and there's an orgy scene as well, though how much of this will be kept in the final version of the film, we don't know . . . it's very strong stuff.'

Already, with the success of *That'll Be The Day* and his two singles *Rock On* and *Lamplight*, David Essex is becoming internationally known and feeling the same strains that Jim Maclaine feels in the film. In an interview with *The Daily Express* in June, 1974, David admitted: 'My wife finds it difficult. My life is filled with things to do. All she has got is a big house with lots of bits in without me. I try and take the family away with me when I can, but there are lots of places where I can't. We find there's a lot of friction between us. It's all in control. We both know it's a difficult situation. I don't think she would love me unless I was that sort of person. She doesn't love me because I'm David Essex. She married me when I was just David Who? . . . if my wife and I woke up one day and found we didn't like our relationship, we would just leave it. I think it's terrible keeping together just because you've got a child. Maureen, my wife, could live without me and I could live without her – even though it would be a shame . . . money is not the driving force. I know I don't have to worry about that any more. The only thing it means to me is artistic freedom . . . success has affected me. I'm not a steady person. I have spasms of complete lunacy. I get wound up to such a pitch I can't come down from it. I used to go crazy in *Godspell* some nights because we had sound difficulties. I would come off and punch people. But I also have moments of complete quietness when I'm totally detached.'

APPENDIX I

CHRONOLOGY

1947
July 23 — David Albert Cook born in Plaistow, East London.

1962
July — Leaves school and becomes an apprentice toolmaker at the Plessey electronic components factory at Ilford.

1963

Joins the Everons as a drummer. Later they change their name to the China Plates Blues Band, and start playing regularly at The Eagle, Chobham Road, London, E.15.

1964
Autumn — The group is signed to management contract by Derek Bowman and his then partner, Stanley Murray.

December — David Cook becomes a solo artist, and changes his name to David Essex.

1965
April — His first record released – *And The Tears Came Tumbling Down/You Can't Stop Me Loving You* (Fontana). Both songs were written by Perry Ford of the Ivy League.

June — Joins Dudley Moore on stage at the Cool Elephant Club and sings *Fly Me To The Moon* and *I'll Remember April*.

December 3	Second single released – *Can't Nobody Love You/Baby, I Don't Mind* (Fontana). The A-side goes to No. 17 in the Radio London chart.
1966	
January 11	Makes his television debut on the children's series *Five O'Clock Club*.
March 25	Third single released – *This Little Girl of Mine/Brokenhearted* (Fontana). Produced by J. J. Jackson.
August 19	Fourth single released – *Thigh High/De Boom Lay Boom* (Fontana).
August 23	Appears again on *Five O'Clock Club*.
October	Starts touring clubs and ballrooms backed by the Stevenage group Mood Indigo.
1967	
April	Signs with Mike Leander at MCA Records.
May	Makes film debut – a 'swinging Londoner' in the film *A Smashing Time* which starred Rita Tushingham and Lyn Redgrave.
May	Joins the actors' trade union Equity, being proposed by Susan Hampshire and Ian McShane.
June	In the United States, MCA release his version of a track from the Beatles' *Sergeant Pepper* album – *She's Leaving Home*, produced by Mike Leander who also arranged the original version for the Beatles. The B-side was *He's A Better Man Than Me*.
November 7	Joins the touring repertory version of *The Fantasticks*.
1968	
May 24	Fifth British single – *Love Story/Higher*

	Than High (on MCA's UNI label), produced by Mike Leander. The A-side was written by Randy Newman.
July 10	Leslie Grade becomes his personal agent after hearing *Love Story*.
October 25	Sixth British single – *Just For Tonight/Goodbye, Goodbye* (Pye). The A-side was written by Tony Macaulay and Barry Mason. Macaulay was also the producer.
December 23	Opens at the Yvonne Arnaud Theatre, Guildford, playing the Sultan in *The Magic Carpet*.

1969

June 6	Seventh British single – *That Takes Me Back/Lost Without Linda* (Decca). Produced by Chris Arnold, David Martin and Geoff Morrow. Decca released the single on the 25th anniversary of D-Day – and commemorated the fact that this was so by distributing 500 toy landing craft to disc jockeys and reviewers!
August/September	Season at La Valbonne, London.
September 26	Eighth British single – *The Day The Earth Stood Still/Is It So Strange?* (Decca).
December	Begins rehearsals as understudy to Tommy Steele as Dick Whittington in London Palladium pantomime.

1970

March 9	Tommy Steele has sore throat – so David gets his chance to play the title at the Palladium. Makes short speech afterwards, and receives seventy fan letters.
March 21	Again plays title role at the Palladium.
July 6	Opens in *Ten Years Hard* with Michael

	Flanders and Sally Smith at the Mayfair Theatre.
September 4	As one half of the duo David and Rozaa, releases *Time of Our Life/We Can Reach An Understanding* (Phillips).
December 17	Opens as Dandini in *Cinderella* at Manchester with Lonnie Donegan as Buttons and Mary Hopkin as Cinderella.

1971

March 13	Releases second record as part of David and Rozaa – *The Spark That Lights The Flame/Two Can Share* (Phillips).
April	Plays a man in a chemist's shop in the film *Assault* which stared Suzy Kendall and Frank Finlay.
August	Plays the part of Ronnie Briggs in the film *All Coppers Are,* and also has small part in the film *Carry On Henry*.
October 13	Chosen from 2,000 candidates for the leading role in the London stage production of *Godspell*.
November 17	*Godspell* opens at the Roundhouse, London.
November 21	In *The Sunday Times*, Harold Hobson writes: 'There are many fine performances now to be seen in London but if I had to choose a single one to show to a visitor it would be this Christ, this simple wondering Christ played by David Essex ...'
December 18	Wife Maureen gives birth to daughter Verity Lee at Ilford Maternity Hospital.

1972

January 26	*Godspell* re-opens at Wyndham's Theatre, London.
February	Bell release the London stage cast version

	of *Godspell* as an album, with David singing on most of the numbers. Tracks: *Save People/Day By Day/Bless The Lord/All For The Best* (on which David played ukelele)*/All Good Gifts/ Light Up The World/Turn Back O Man/Alas For You/We Beseech Thee.*
February 27	Harold Hobson again reviews *Godspell* in *The Sunday Times*, and writes: 'It is my firm opinion that Mr. Essex's is the best performance in London, the happiest and the most moving. That it should be so at a time when we all marvel at Olivier's prestigious James Tyrone, one of our greatest actors' finest creations, is a measure of Mr. Essex's achievement.'
June 18	Appears in *The Box Office Christ* (BBC-1) with Bishop Trevor Huddleston and Tim Rice, who co-wrote *Jesus Christ, Superstar.*
October 23	Given seven-week leave from *Godspell* to begin filming *That'll Be The Day* on the Isle of Wight with Ringo Starr, Billy Fury, Keith Moon, etc.

1973
January 28	Appears in Gala Matinee to raise funds for the Sunshine Fund for Blind Babies.
April 12	David and his wife Maureen attend the world première of *That'll Be The Day* at the ABC-2 Theatre, Shaftesbury Avenue, London. Ronco release the soundtrack LP of the film.
April 28	Appears on *The John Denver Show* (BBC-2).
May 13	Begins four-week BBC-1 series *What Shall We Tell The Children?* reading

	stories written by Spike Milligan, and singing songs with a group of children.
May 19	Attends Variety Club Star Gala at Battersea.
May 24	Selects favourite records on *My Top 12* (Radio One).
May 27	After concert by Paul McCartney and *Wings* at Hammersmith Odeon, David and Maureen attend party at Cafè Royal, Regent Street, along with Marc Bolan, Rod Stewart, Elton John, Paul and Linda McCartney, Keith Richards, Charlie Watts, Cat Stevens, etc.
June 24	Plays in charity cricket match at the Oval with Leslie Crowther, Henry Cooper, Ed Stewart and Brian Rix.
August 7	Tours London record shops as part of CBS promotion.
August 10	Releases the first songs he has written himself – *Rock on/On and On* (CBS) produced by Jeff Wayne, formerly arranger for the *Righteous Brothers*.
August 10	Chaos in Bond Street when 1,000 fans turn up for his personal appearance at Chappell's music store.
August 16	Reception at Quaglino's to celebrate the release of *Rock On* and his signing five-year recording contract with CBS Records.
August 26	Appears on *Russell Harty Plus* (London Weekend TV).
September 15	Leaves *Godspell*.
September 22	*Rock On* reaches No. 1 in the British Charts.
September 23	Appears on *Ask Aspel* (BBC-1).
October 17	Films for NBC TV *Midnight Special* series aboard boat *Windsor*, with fans

	invited to join the trip at Westminster Pier.
October 18	Flies to Holland to film *Top Pop* TV series.
October 20	Paris for TV.
October 22	Flies on to Munich and then Frankfurt and Bremen for further TV promotional appearances.
October 31	Returns to London.
November 2	Second CBS single released, again with both tracks written by David and produced by Jeff Wayne – *Lamplight/We All Insane*.
November 2	First LP released by CBS, titled *Rock On* and again produced by Jeff Wayne. Seven tracks (marked *) written by David. Tracks: *Lamplight*/Turn Me Loose/On and On*/Streetfight*/Rock On*/Ocean Girl*/Bring In The Sun/For Emily, Wherever I May Find Her/We All Insane*/Tell Him No/September 15th**.
November 23	Seen in US on *Midnight Special* (NBC TV) with Bee Gees and Gilbert O'Sullivan.
November 25	David flies to US to begin personal appearances at special press showings of *That'll Be The Day*.
November 26	New York.
November 27	Phoenix.
November 28	Los Angeles.
November 29	San Francisco.
November 30	Seattle, and another appearance on *Midnight Special* (NBC TV).
December 1	Denver.
December 3	Houston.
December 4	Dallas.

December 5	Fort Worth.
December 6	Philadelphia.
December 7	Boston.
December 8	New York.
December 9	Returns from US and says at London Airport that he has turned down offers that would have meant living in the States.
December 13/14	Appears as the Narrator in stage version of *Tommy* at the Rainbow Theatre, London.
December 26	Guests on *Sez Lez* (Yorkshire TV).
December 31	Wins Variety Club Award as Most Promising Newcomer of 1973.

1974
January 2	Ringo Starr announces that he has refused to appear in film follow-up to *That'll Be The Day* – *Stardust*. 'Having lived through the madness once, I couldn't experience it a second time. It's too close to home.'
January 5	David flies to the United States and films two appearances on *The Phil Everly Show* (ABC TV), two for *Midnight Special* (NBC TV) and two for *Action – Dick Clark* (ABC TV).
February 16	Wins *Disc and Music Echo* award as the Brightest Hope for 1974.
February 18	*Stardust* goes into production in London before location-shooting in a Spanish castle and in Manchester, and in the States. The production schedule is nine weeks.
February 21/22	David talks about his East End childhood in a two-part BBC-1 schools programme based on Arthur Morrison's book *A Child Of The Jago*.

March 5	*Rock On* receives the annual *New Musical Express* award as the Best British Produced Pop Record, and CBS wins the award for the Best British Marketing Concept.
March 14	*Rock On* reaches No. 1 in the US Chart organised by the trade magazine *Cashbox*.
March 17	David appears in mock concert staged at Belle Vue, Manchester, for the filming of *Stardust*. Members of his fan club are allowed in free – for others the tickets are 40p. He is guarded by forty security guards – and thirty girls faint. The producers say this one scene the film has cost £25,000.
March 28	Wins US Gold Disc from the Recording Industry Association of America for 1,000,000 US dollar sales of *Rock On*.
April 10	*That'll Be The Day* released in major US cities with *Rock On* now dubbed over the closing credits.
April 18	*Lamplight* released in the US.
April 27	Leaves for the US to continue filming *Stardust*.
May	Although not a major success in Britain, *America/Dance Little Girl* is a huge hit in France – where David appears in the top TV shows *Domino* and *Top à Dalida*.
May 3	Third CBS single released – *America/Dance Little Girl*, again with both tracks written by David, and with production by Jeff Wayne.
May/June	Records his second album with producer Jeff Wayne.
June/August	Rents a country house near St. Tropez, France, staying there with his family – and writing songs.

August 31	Of his forthcoming British tour, his first-ever as a recording star, David tells *Disc and Music Echo*: 'They wanted me to do two shows in Bristol and I said only if I can do East Ham Granada!'
September 19	Press conference at the Café Royal, London, to announce his album, his single and tour plans.
September 27	CBS release the single *Gonna Make You A Star/Window* which subsequently reaches No. 1 in all the British music paper charts. CBS release the album *David Essex*. Tracks: *Gonna Make You A Star/Window/I Know/There's Something About You Baby/Good Ol' Rock and Roll/America/Dance Little Girl/Ooh Darling/Little Miss Sweetness/Stardust*
October 12	David tells the *Daily Express* that he found making *Stardust* was 'three months of agony' because he started to become the character he was playing and 'a sort of arrogance crept into me'.
October 24	London première for *Stardust*.
November 1	David begins his first concert tour at Southampton Gaumont, with his record producer Jeff Wayne as musical director. The supporting acts are Merlin and Batti MamZelle
November 2	East Ham Granada
November 3	Cardiff Capitol
November 5	Bristol Hippodrome
November 6	Hanley Victoria Hall
November 8	Sheffield City Hall
November 9	Manchester Free Trade Hall
November 9	Reviewing his concert act, a *Melody Maker* critic says 'he proved himself to

	be Britain's answer to David Cassidy.'
November 10	Birmingham Hippodrome.
November 11	Liverpool Empire – 5,000 fans block the streets around the theatre.
November 12	Edinburgh Usher Hall.
November 13	Glasgow Apollo.
November 15	Newcastle City Hall.
November 16	Stockton Globe.
November 17	Ipswich Gaumont.
November 18	Bournemouth Winter Gardens.
November 19	Hastings White Rock Pavilion.
November 21	Portsmouth Guildhall.
November 23	Brighton Dome.
November 24	Lewisham Odeon.
November 25	Preston Guildhall.
November 26	Blackpool Opera House.
November 27	Sutton Granada.
November 28	Oxford New Theatre.
November 29	Swansea Brangwyn Hall.
November 30	Taunton Odeon.
December 2/7	Appears all week at the New Victoria Theatre, London, with every performance sold out, and even extra concerts sold out.
December 7	His last performance at the New Victoria Theatre is recorded live for a possible live LP.
December 13	Fans block Regent Street when he visits BBC Broadcasting House to appear on a radio show.
	CBS release single *Stardust/Miss Sweetness*.
December 16	Flies to Paris for two concerts at the Olympia.

1975
January 4   The *New Musical Express* reports that David Essex has become the biggest seller

	on the CBS record label in ten years, and is expected to have a straight dramatic role in his next film, with his only music being the theme song over the credits.
January	Flies to the US for a TV special with Olivia Newton-John.
January 29	Attends the US première of *Stardust* in Boston, and then begins a tour of US cities appearing at gala openings of the film.

APPENDIX II

Cast List and Synopsis for
'THAT'LL BE THE DAY'

This was the first of the two films in which David Essex played the role of a young teenager Jim Maclaine who grew up in the fifties, rejected the chance of furthering his education, drifted instead of choosing a career, rebelled against the standards set by his parents, and eventually turned to rock 'n' roll. In the first film, this was the cast:

Jim Maclaine	DAVID ESSEX
Mike	RINGO STARR
Mrs Maclaine	ROSEMARY LEACH
Mr Maclaine	JAMES BOOTH
Stormy Tempest	BILLY FURY
J. D. Clover	KEITH MOON
Jeannette	ROSALIND AYRES
Terry	ROBERT LINDSAY
Jean	BETH MORRIS
Grandad	JAMES OTTAWAY
Wendy	VERNA HARVEY
Joan	ERIN GERAGHTY
Sandra	DEBORAH WATLING
Sandra's friend	PATTI LOVE
Mrs Sutcliffe	DAPHNE OXENFORD
Mr Sutcliffe	BERNARD SEVERN
Charlotte	KIM BRADEN
Jack	JOHNNY SHANNON
Girls in Coffee bar	SUSAN HOLDERNESS
	SALLY WATTS
Johnny Swinburn	KARL HOWMAN
Doreen	BRENDA BRUCE
Schoolteacher	ALAN FOSS

Young girl at fair	PATSY BLOWER
Girl with baby	SARA CLEE
Young Jim	SACHA PATTNAM

CREDITS

Directed by	CLAUDE WHATHAM
Produced by	DAVID PUTTNAM and SANFORD LIEBERSON
Original story and screenplay by	RAY CONNOLLY
Executive producer	ROY BAIRD
Photographed by	PETER SUSCHITZKY
Music supervised by	NEIL ASPINALL and KEITH MOON
Additional material scored by	WILL MALONE
Editor	MICHAEL BRADSELL
Sound Editor	IAN FULLER
Art Director	BRIAN MORRIS
Costume Consultant	RUTH MYERS
Assistant Director	GARTH THOMAS

SYNOPSIS

Jim Maclaine (DAVID ESSEX) is a dark, good-looking schoolboy of 18 who is studying for his advanced level examinations at school in Britain in 1958. At least, he's supposed to be studying but, unlike his more studious and serious best friend Terry Sutcliffe (ROBERT LINDSAY), Jim finds his book-work increasingly irksome. He's intelligent enough and finds his school studies easy to cope with. But he feels that a further two or three years at university followed by 'a safe' career would be dull.

So it is that on his way to take his final exams with Terry, Jim throws his books and school cap into the river with a scathing, 'I've had enough of sodding school . . .' and cycles back home.

'Home' is a small house and general grocer's shop run by Jim's mother, Mrs Maclaine (ROSEMARY LEACH). The only other occupant is his grandfather, since Tim's own father grew restless soon after his return from the war and walked out on his family. Now Jim resolves to walk out too and, after packing a suitcase with a few clothes (plus pictures of his idols James Dean and Elvis Presley), he hitches a lift to a seaside resort and moves into a seedy bed-sitting room. Soon he has a job as a deck-chair attendant on the beach and revels in his so-called freedom. When his mother visits him and asks him to return home he refuses – but asks if she will send him record player and records. Terry duly delivers them and is aghast at Jim's present situation.

Next Jim works as a bar assistant in a seaside holiday camp, with his new-found friend Mike (RINGO STARR), who is a rough looking boy whose main topic of conversation is sex. They share a camp chalet and plan to meet all the girls they can.

After their spell with the holiday camp, Mike and Jim get work at a fairground, where Mike has worked regularly before. They continue to get all the girls they want and they make a useful side-profit by short-changing the customers. One day Mike picks on a member of a gang of 'Teddy Boys' to swindle and is later severely beaten up.

Jim's old friend Terry visits the fair and invites Jim to accompany him to a dance being held at his university's Students Union building (Terry is now studying for a degree and leading the sort of academic life that Jim has opted out of). Jim finds the atmosphere and people there irritating and 'square'. But at the same time he feels 'left out'.

Jim is so affected by this experience that he leaves the fairground and returns home to live with his mother and grandfather. He has a much-needed hair cut, buys better clothes and helps in his mother's shop, even putting up a new sign and buying a van. He meets again Terry's younger sister Jeannette (ROSALIND AYRES), sees her with new eyes and, after a whirlwind courtship, marries her – though a touch of the old Jim manifests itself when he spends his last bachelor night sleeping with Jeannette's best friend and bridesmaid, Jean (BETH MORRIS). After a year or so Jim and Jeannette celebrate the birth of their baby and everything seems happy and settled – on the surface. In reality, Jim is becoming bored and suffocated by his new 'respectable' life, the sort of life he has always scorned. He is becoming more and more obsessed with pop music and takes every opportunity to attend pop concerts.

When Jim bumps into an old school friend who is now a successful semi-professional pop group leader, he makes up his mind. Like his father before him he leaves his wife (and his mother, with whom he and Jeannette and their baby have been living), coldly walking out on his 'respectability' in search once again of freedom and irresponsibility.

We last see him as he buys a guitar from a music store, obviously having resolved to try his hand at a career in pop music. 'Sure you'll be able to handle it?' enquires the shop assistant. 'I'll be alright . . .' affirms Jim. He will be . . .

As well as releasing details of the cast and synopsis, Anglo-EMI (who distributed the film) issued these brief biographical sketches of the film's stars:–

DAVID ESSEX
'If it hadn't been for music I'd probably be in gaol by now.' The speaker: dark, good-looking, 25-year-old David Essex, who has won remarkable critical and public acclaim for his performance as Jesus Christ in the London production of the American religious rock musical *Godspell*, and who now stars in *That'll Be The Day*. Today he's a sought-after stage star and about to become a movie star. But he hasn't always had it so good.

David admits that his childhood and upbringing in the East End of London was rough – and tough. David's father was a docker, money was short, and David went to a local secondary modern school which wasn't exactly on a par with Eton College.

'My schooldays were pretty violent, I suppose,' he reflects. 'The police used to come round the classrooms at the end of each term to search us all for weapons. I was a real little tearaway and always on the verge of being expelled. I remember setting fire to the science laboratory once. Then, another time, two or three of us gassed the biology master's bees – that was a nasty thing to do and I was sorry afterwards. The master set about me with his cane and it was all very scary! The best teachers always tried to avoid taking our class.

'Then I was in a tough street gang and had lots of fights. I was beaten up one night by a rival gang when they spotted me out by myself. That was all a bit like *West Side Story* – except that it should have been called *East End Story*.

'I worked on a fairground that used to come every year, too. I jumped on and off the dodgem-cars, collecting fares and chatting up the girls. I loved the colour and life of the fairground, it was a special sort of world. I used to show off a bit, I suppose. But the fairground world's a bit like the showbiz world, when you think about it. Anyway, working the dodgems made me feel "somebody" while I was there and most young people like to feel that they're "somebody", don't they?

'Some of the lads I was at school with have ended up as crooks, which is rather sad. But I always loved music and when I spotted a drum-kit in a local shop-window one day I wanted it more than anything else at that moment. My father eventually bought it for me, just to keep me quiet, I think! So I practised like mad and when I was 14 I was playing drums with blues bands in pubs and clubs. I sang a bit, too.

'I made a few records, but it didn't mean a thing. So then I went into various stage repertory companies and toured around in plays and shows. I was 18 and learning fast. You really learn how to act by making mistakes up there on the stage. Any one can learn to act, really. If they can laugh and cry, they can act. It's all to do with the emotions.

'This part I've got in *That'll Be The Day* – Jim Maclaine – I identify quite a lot with him. He leaves home at about 18 and I went at 19. Jim opted out of the academic or apprenticeship roads to success and so did I. He wants to be free and unfettered and so did I. I still do. I think a lot of people are going to see something of themselves in Jim when they see the film. If they're in their teens now, they'll know exactly what he goes through because a lot of them will be going through the same sort of thing themselves. And the older people who see it will look back, not with anger, but maybe with a touch of sadness and nostalgia. And certainly with understanding.'

BILLY FURY

Billy Fury – Britain's rock 'n' roll answer to America's Elvis Presley in the late 1950's and early-1960's – makes his motion picture come-back in *That'll Be The Day*. And makes it with remarkable success.

Billy appears in the film, set in that time – his own period – as the leader of a pop group called Stormy Tempest and the Typhoons playing at a holiday camp. As Stormy, Billy performs a couple of typical rock numbers of the period in his usual energetic, hip-swivelling, lip-curling style, remembered so well from his appearances in TV shows and in his previous films *Play It Cool* and *I Gotta Horse*. Billy's chart-topping records in those days included *Halfway to Paradise, I'll Never Find Another You, Jealousy, Margo* and *Collette*.

Although Billy Fury, now 31, doesn't appear in the record-charts or on TV these days, he still does many shows throughout Great Britain, in clubs and on 'one-night stands', still drawing huge audiences wherever he appears. His career suffered a temporary set-back a couple of years ago when he was ill, and had to take things easily. But he confesses to enjoying this new slower tempo and devotes much of his spare time to his hobby of ornithology and, in particular, of photographing birds. He hopes to publish a book of his bird pictures shortly. Today he lives in Surrey, where another hobby is the breeding of Welsh mountain ponies.

In his role as Stormy Tempest in *That'll Be The Day*, Billy heads a group which comprises several famed pop musicians of today, including Keith Moon (of *The Who*), Graham Bond and John Hawkins. Watched by 150 extras, Billy Fury (in silver glitter jacket and black satin trousers) sang a catchy number titled *Long Live Rock* for one sequence and it was some time before the applauding, cheering fans could be silenced by the assistant directors so that the number could be shot again. As somebody remarked: 'Billy just never gets any older – and his style still makes him this country's Number One rock performer.' With the 1950's nostalgia wave reaching its height, there could be an old name at the top of the record charts when *That'll Be The Day* is released: The name of Billy Fury.

RINGO STARR

There's only one Ringo in show business and he's every inch a Starr. So maybe the joke's been made before but it makes as good a lead-in as any to a brief glance at the ex-Beatle and his remarkable career to date, who now co-stars with David Essex and Rosemary Leach in the new film production *That'll Be The Day*. Ringo Starr is seen in a straight, dramatic role, laced with earthy humour, unusual for someone who has rarely been seen without a pair of drumsticks in his hands over the past ten years or so. But that seems to be the new trend for Ringo. He has already made three films as an actor, as opposed to a pop musician, and is growing to like this relatively new career. 'I enjoy the acting bit and would like to do more, if the right sort of parts come along,' he says in those still strong Liverpudlian tones. Chances are that the right parts will come along after his striking portrayal of Mike – colleague, mate and sexual adviser to Jim (played by David Essex) in *That'll Be The Day*.

Mike is a fairly typical, greasy-haired, sex-mad, cynical, Teddy-boy-suited lad of the late-1950's in the film. Easy-going, taking life as it comes, proud of his small prowesses in dancing, drinking, fiddling and girl-laying, Mike works with Jim first as a barman in a holiday camp, then as a money-collector on the rides in a fairground.

It's an acting performance that is going to surprise a lot of Ringo's pop fans with its gritty realism and evidence of a genuine dramatic flair.

Ringo Starr was born Richard Starkey in Dingle, Liverpool, on July 7, 1940, and was educated at St. Silas's Primary School (where a fellow-pupil was one Ronnie Wycherley – later to win fame as Billy Fury. Later he attended Dingle Vale Secondary Modern School, where he excelled at handicraft lessons, even if he didn't shine in subjects such as mathematics and science.

Watching his talent at creating finely-fashioned objects in wood, and observing his delicately-sensitive hands and fingers, his teachers suggested that he might learn to play a musical instrument. Ringo wasn't particularly enthusiastic – until his parents gave him a drum-kit (price £10) as a Christmas present. He immediately found that he had a flair for drumming and for rhythm – especially for a uniquely fierce style of percussive pounding! He couldn't practise at school but used to get into trouble for drumming on his classroom desk with his fingers!

When he left school, Ringo was interested in a career in either motor-racing or hairdressing. But, as drumming swiftly turned into a full-time occupation, he soon forgot both. In fact his earliest jobs were as a messenger boy for British Rail and as a barman on the Liverpool–North Wales ferryboat.

In 1960 he began to play regularly with the Eddie Clayton Skiffle Group, also playing with the Dark Town Skiffle Group. Then, from 1960–62, Ringo played drums with Rory Storm and the Hurricanes, including three seasons at a holiday camp.

Ringo had first met John Lennon, Paul McCartney and George Harrison in 1960 at the Kaiser Keller, Hamburg, when he was appearing there with Rory Storm. He didn't appear with them until the following year when he would occasionally sit in and drum with them at the famous Liverpool Cavern. Then, in 1962, Ringo left Rory Storm and joined The Beatles (as Lennon, McCartney and Harrison were now calling themselves) in place of Pete Best on drums. The Beatles' first record *Love Me Do* was released in October, 1962. It was a success and was followed early in 1963 with a second single, *Please Please Me*. It was an immediate hit, won a million-plus new fans for The Beatles and resulted in them touring Britain, appearing on television and radio, and collecting a Silver Disc. Their next records *From Me To You* and *Twist and Shout* (with Lennon's dynamic singing solo) really established the group and, as they say, the rest is history.

The Beatles' influence on the pop music world – and young people everywhere – was, as many said, one of the biggest of this century. And apart from their fame as a group, they won individual acclaim too, not least Ringo. He became probably the most famous and talented drummer of his generation. Ringo also sang, of course, with the Beatles, scoring hits with vocal solos.

The last LP on which The Beatles all played together before their dissolution was *Let it Be* in 1970. In 1971 Ringo composed and recorded the million-seller hit single *It Don't Come Easy*.

Among Ringo's motion picture appearances have been *A Hard Day's Night* (1964), *Help!* (1965) and *Let It Be* (1970) (all with The Beatles), and *Candy* (1968), *The Magic Christian* (1969) and *Count Downe* (1972), which he also produced for Apple Films, of which he is also managing director.

Ringo's name, incidentally, stems from the collection of striking rings which he used to wear on the fingers of both hands.

Ringo married Maureen Cox in February, 1965, and today they live in London with their three young children: Jason, Zak and daughter Lee. Ringo's spare-time hobbies include designing furniture and light-fittings, photography, swimming, and being with his family.

Ringo Starr maintains his second-to-none reputation as a superlative drummer and musician. Now he consolidates his new career as dramatic screen actor with his memorable performance in *That'll Be The Day*.

RINGO TALKS:—

'I really enjoy film acting and want to do more of it. I like the whole fantasy of it all – being someone else, you know.

I'd really love to do a costume picture – that's the ultimate fantasy. Something like *The Three Musketeers* or *The Knights of the Round Table* where I could wear a suit of armour and do a bit of sword-fighting – that'd be fantastic.

'Another thing I'd like to make is a silent movie. No words at all, just action and music and sound effects. Rita Tushingham would be marvellous in a silent picture – she's got such a visual face. I'd really like to try that.

'Of course another reason a silent picture would be great is the fact that I wouldn't have any words to learn! It's the words that get in the way all the time in many films. The most difficult things I find about filming are learning the lines and getting up early!

'The best film part I've ever had is in a picture called *Blind Man*. I play a Mexican. I get to rape the girl, stab her father, beat up someone up and so on. It was really a great part and a good scene for me.

'My part as Mike in *That'll Be The Day* is total flashback for me personally, since he's very much me as I was in the late-fifties. Mike's worked on a ferry-boat, as a barman and in a holiday-camp, and so did I. He's a Liverpudlian and so am I. There are lots of other affinities as well. So I feel very much at home in the part – especially as I also wrote my scenes with Ray Connolly, who did the script.

'Another coincidence is that Billy Fury appears in *That'll Be The Day*. Billy and I were in the same class at School in Dingle, Liverpool.

'People usually seem to offer me comedy sort of film parts, where I make everyone laugh – the sort of perpetual "Happy Clown" – but I'm trying to get away from all that. It's too easy. Anyone can pull a funny face. The more dramatic roles are better for me, I think. In *That'll Be The Day* I exit from the film after being beaten-up by a gang of tough Teddy-boys. That's pretty dramatic. I've still got the bruises to prove it...!

'I'm a bit of a Teddy-boy myself in the film. I even wear my own actual velvet-collared Ted jacket which I wore around the late-'50's. Everyone reeled back from the smell of mothballs when I put it on! I wear a pair of socks I used to wear in those days too.

'I used to go to the pictures twice, or even three times, every week as a lad. I really enjoyed most types of films, but liked plenty of action. My hero in those days was Victor Mature. He was tough and likeable – a guy for the lads of 15 to look up to. For years I've admired people like Elizabeth Taylor, Marlon Brando, Burt Lancaster and Fred Astaire. They never give bad performances. It was a big kick for me to meet them when I was out in Hollywood.

The really big people are always the greatest. It's the one-shot characters who can be nasty. Like the people who make one record and then go crazy and think they're the greatest thing ever to hit show-biz. Deep down they know they've got no real talent and that they've had a lucky break. Then they get into a sort of paranoic state because they can't do it again.

'I've been branching out a bit lately. I produced *Count Downe*, as well as appearing in it as Merlin the Magician. And I produced, directed and appeared in another film titled *Born to Boogie*, with Marc Bolan, T. Rex and Elton John. I really dug directing, it's the greatest scene ever for me. These two pictures I made for Apple Films, of which I'm Managing Director. That sounds very grand – but I suppose it is!'

KEITH MOON

Keith Moon. If you've heard of contemporary pop you've heard of Keith Moon. He is – and has been since the group's inception in the early 1960's – the drummer with The Who and, consequently an essential and integral part of this mind-bending, sensational pop group. With The Beatles and The Rolling Stones, probably the most influential pop combination of modern times. The Who's hits, and they're many, include such titles as *My Generation, Substitute, I'm A Boy, I Can See For Miles* and the highly-rated rock opera *Tommy*. And the percussive talents of Moon have been involved with them all.

Now Keith Moon makes a special guest appearance in *That'll Be The Day*. His role: J. D. Clover, drummer with the fictional pop group specially formed for the picture, Stormy Tempest and the Typhoons. Billy Fury is the rock singing Stormy while the rest of the group includes Graham Bond (saxophone) and John Hawkins (piano).

Keith pounds the vellum in his usual brilliant, violent style and also shows a new and natural acting talent in his brief, but effective, appearances in the film, revealing hilarious, eye-rolling flair. He also has a brand-new image, since his hitherto long dark hair has been specially cut short into a 1950's-style for his role. 'It feels a bit strange, but it makes a change . . .', he grins amiably.

Keith was so enthusiastic during a lengthy drum-break in the picture, that he broke no fewer than three drumsticks in the process! 'If a thing's worth doing, it's worth doing well,' he commented.

He has previously appeared in Frank Zappa's film *200 Motels* – in the role of a nun! – and more or less as himself in *Count Downe* with his old mate Ringo Starr (who also produced), but in a straight dramatic part and without a drumstick in sight. In the evenings back at their hotel in the Isle of Wight (where the picture was made entirely on location), the two pop stars got together, and made sweet, if noisy music, for the entertainment of the rest of the cast and crew. 'I love drumming, it's part of my life,' says Keith. He adds: 'I'd like to do more acting – I enjoy it a lot.'

Today Keith Moon lives in a fabulous highly-futuristic house at Chertsey in Surrey. The residence is impossible to describe fully, but basically comprises a huge pyramid with smaller pyramids at each corner. There is little conventional furniture but in the main 'living room' pyramid there is a sunken 'conversation pit' lined with leather banquette seats with a television set which disappears into the floor at the touch of a switch.

Keith's cars include a lilac-coloured Rolls Royce (complete with TV set), a white Mercedes, a white AC428 (with stereo sound), a Morgan Plus 8, a war-time Chrysler V8, a Beach Buggy, and – the *pièce de résistance* – an 'Air Cycle' hover-

craft which he bought from Los Angeles and finds useful for
'popping down to the local pub'. So far, Keith hasn't got a car
fitted with a drum kit, but that can only be a matter of time.

ROSALIND AYRES

Rosalind Ayres was born in Birmingham on December 7th
1946. In 1968 she spent a year working as assistant stage
manager and small part actress at a repertory theatre. The
following year she appeared in various television productions
and then toured the United States with the Royal Shakespeare
Company, understudying Sara Kestelmann as Titania in *A
Midsummer Night's Dream* (and playing the role twice in
Boston).

In 1972 she made her London West End stage debut at the
Queen's Theatre as Calpurnia in *I, Claudius*, also making her
film debut in *The Lovers*. Her many TV appearances include
those in *Family At War*, *The Lovers*, *Coronation Street*, *Home
And Away*, *General Hospital* and several drama productions.
In *That'll Be The Day* she plays Jeannette, the pretty, likeable girl who marries Jim (David Essex) and hopes, vainly,
that he will settle down into a quiet home life with her and
their baby.

ROSEMARY LEACH

Rosemary Leach was born on December 18th, 1935, the
daughter of school-teachers. After studying at The Royal
Academy of Dramatic Art, in London, she appeared with
repertory companies all over Britain. She made her television
bow in 1961 and, over the past few years, has become one of
Britain's most popular and widely-hailed TV actresses. In 1965
she was runner-up for the Best Actress of the Year Award,
presented by the Television's Producer's Guild. Her numerous
TV appearances include those in *The Power Game*, *Roads To
Freedom*, *The Wild Duck*, *Germinal* and the acclaimed TV
version of Laurie Lee's *Cider With Rosie* (in which she played
the mother). This production was also directed by Claude
Whatham, director of *That'll Be The Day*. For her perfor-

mance in *Cider With Rosie*, Rosemary Leach received a nomination as Best TV Actress of the Year, 1971. She recently finished appearing in a major TV film version of *Don Quixote* with Rex Harrison and Frank Finlay.

In *That'll Be The Day*, Rosemary Leach is seen as Mrs Maclaine, Jim's long-suffering and resigned mother.

CLAUDE WHATHAM – DIRECTOR

Claude Whatham was born in Manchester on December 2nd, 1935. After studying theatre design, he worked as resident designer with several repertory companies. He was invited by Granada TV to join their design team and soon afterwards took the company's Directors' course, emerging as a fully-fledged television director. His first major production was Anouilh's *The Lark*, which starred Nicol Williamson. This was followed by a wide variety of plays.

In 1966 Claude Whatham joined the BBC and directed several plays including John Mortimer's *A Voyage Round My Father*, which Mortimer originally wrote for TV. This production won Whatham a Nomination for a Society of Film and TV Arts Award and he also directed the first stage production of this play. He later directed *The Lions Cub*, the first episode of *Elizabeth R*, starring Glenda Jackson; it was this episode which won an 'Emmy' for the Outstanding Single Programme of 1971–72 (separately from Miss Jackson's own two awards). Next came his production of Laurie Lee's *Cider With Rosie*, which was seen on BBC TV at Christmas 1971 and repeated in September, 1972, receiving rave reviews and public acclaim.

His most recent production is the serial of Colette's book *Cheri*, which was seen on BBC TV in the spring of 1973. *That'll Be The Day* marks Claude Whatham's directorial debut in the motion picture sphere.

ROY BAIRD – EXECUTIVE PRODUCER

Roy Baird started in the film industry as a third assistant director. Most recently he has acted as associate producer on the Ken Russell films *Women In Love* and *The Devils* and as executive producer on *The Music Lovers*. In 1971 he produced the highly-successful film *Henry VIII and His Six Wives*.

RAY CONNOLLY – WRITER
Ray Connolly is a columnist with the London *Evening Standard*. Brought up in Lancashire he gained an honours degree in Social Anthropology from the London School of Economics in 1963, beginning a career in journalism with the *Liverpool Daily Post* the following year.

That'll Be The Day is his first screenplay. In March 1973 his first novel, *A Girl Who Came To Stay*, was published.

Aged 33, he is married, has three children and lives in Kensington.

SANFORD LIEBERSON – PRODUCER
Sanford Lieberson was born in California in 1936. His first job was in Public Relations after which he embarked on a successful career in the film and theatrical agency field both in America and Europe. In 1968 he became a producer with the film *Performance*. In 1969 he joined David Puttnam when they formed a television cassette company.

DAVID PUTTNAM – PRODUCER
Born in London in 1941, David Puttnam left school at seventeen to work in advertising. At the age of twenty-five he formed his own agency to represent photographers and within two years this had become the biggest company of its type in the world. A year after that, together with Sanford Lieberson, he formed a company to exploit the possibilities of cassette television.

David Puttnam has previously produced *Melody*, starring Mark Lester, and *The Pied Piper of Hamelin* directed by Jacques Demy, starring Donovan and Jack Wild.

APPENDIX III
Cast List and Synopsis for
STARDUST

In *Stardust*, David Essex continues the role of Jim Maclaine – and the film follows his career as a top rock superstar in the sixties. This was the cast list: –

Jim Maclaine	DAVID ESSEX
Mike	ADAM FAITH
Porter Lee Austin	LARRY HAGMAN
J. D. Clover	KEITH MOON
Colin Day	MARTY WILDE
Johnny	PAUL NICHOLAS
Alex	DAVE EDMUNDS
Danielle	INES DES LONGCHAMPS
Stevie	KARL HOWMAN
Kevin	PETER DUNCAN
Harrap	JOHN NORMINGTON
Felix Hoffman	RICK LEE PARMENTIER
Jeannette	ROSALIND AYRES
Brian	JAMES HAZELDINE
Ralph Woods	MICHAEL ELPHICK
Linda (twin)	CLAIRE RUSSELL
Polly (twin)	BOBBY SPARROW

INTRODUCTION
'*Stardust* is an attempt to make the definitive, fictionalised film of the creation, rise and fall of any one of the top rock superstars of the 1960's. And it is as authentic as we man possibly make it.'

The speaker: David Puttnam, co-producer of a new motion picture titled *Stardust*, in which David Essex re-creates the role of Jim Maclaine, the rebellious anti-hero of *That'll Be*

The Day, pound-for-pound the most successful film of 1973 in the UK.

Stardust also stars Adam Faith and Larry Hagman, with Keith Moon, Marty Wilde, Paul Nicholas and Dave Edmunds, and introduces lovely French actress Ines des Longchamps.

The Goodtimes Enterprises Production, for distribution by EMI FILM Distributors Ltd., is directed from Ray Connolly's original screenplay by Michael Apted. He has been responsible for many top-ranking television productions and made his motion picture debut in 1972 when he directed the widely-acclaimed *The Triple Echo*, starring Glenda Jackson and Oliver Reed.

Stardust has the same production team as *That'll Be The Day*: it is produced by David Puttnam and Sandy Lieberson, with Roy Baird as executive producer and Gavrik Losey as associate producer. Ray Connolly also wrote the screenplay of *That'll Be The Day*, which came tenth in the list of the most successful money-making films of 1973 in the UK. The film also won for David Essex the Variety Club of Great Britain's 'Most Promising Newcomer Of The Year' Award, plus other awards and plaudits. Essex's success in *That'll Be The Day*, in his two-year spell playing the leading role in the London stage production of *Godspell*, and with his recent record hits (including *Rock On* and *Lamplight*) have made him one of the most exciting and likeable new talents on the international show business scene.

One of the leading stars of the early-sixties was Adam Faith, so he is only too familiar with the authentic pop world portrayed by *Stardust*. In the film, he plays Mike, the shrewd, sardonic personal manager who helps Jim Maclaine to the top. Faith has recently scored successes as a 'straight' actor in various stage productions and in the successful TV series *Budgie*, which won him a whole new public. He is also busy composing, and record-producing with his new recording discovery Leo Sayer.

Keith Moon, famous drummer with The Who, repeats his zany portrayal of J. D. Clover, whom he created in *That'll Be*

The Day. Clover is the drummer with the Stray Cats, the pop group headed by Jim Maclaine in *Stardust*.

Marty Wilde was, of course, a contemporary pop star of Adam Faith's and he continues to make successful appearances up and down Britain. In the film he plays Colin Day, the first 'big-time' agent to Maclaine and his group.

Paul Nicholas starred in the original London production of *Hair*, then went on to star in the title-role of the original London production of *Jesus Christ, Superstar*, and is currently starring in *Grease* on the London stage. Dave Edmunds has had three hit single records in the past year – *I Hear You Knocking*, *Be My Baby* and *Born To Be With You* and has produced the music recordings for *Stardust*. In the film, Paul Nicholas plays Johnny and Dave Edmunds plays Alex – both members of The Stray Cats.

Ines des Longchamps is a beautiful young French actress who plays the role of Danielle, Jim Maclaine's loyal but troubled girl-friend. Others in the talented cast include Rosalined Ayres, John Normington, Karl Howman, James Hazeldine and Peter Duncan.

The world of pop music in the 1960s portrayed in *Stardust* will bring back memories for anyone who was in any way involved in it, either as participant or spectator, and create new ones for those who weren't.

It is a world of one-night-stands with two-a-night 'groupie girls', eager to harmonize with the pop-groups; of dates in seedy small-town clubs where the girls dance with each other and with their fantasies: of bed-and-no-breakfast in the back of a van; of broken promises and false premises (or vice versa). It's a world in which a microphone becomes the centre of the universe and in which an amplified guitar echoes shatteringly even in your dreams.

When we last saw Jim Maclaine in *That'll Be The Day*, he had just opted out of suburban domestic marriage and fatherhood, and was buying a guitar. Now, when we first see him in *Stardust*, he is a singer-guitarist with a not-very-successful group called The Stray Cats. When Mike Menarry

(Adam Faith) joins them as road manager, things begin to look up and they get a wealthy bachelor's patronage. Then comes the big-time, a string of hit records, international tours, American homage – and superstar success for Jim, is fêted and mobbed wherever he goes. This is the bitter-sweet world of excess as well as success, where a slipped disc isn't a physical ailment but a financial one and where stardust can turn to tardust overnight. A world where a string of luxury hotel suites is home and where you're as relaxed as a high-wire-trapese artist condemned to walk the tight-rope forever. Until you fall off with exhaustion. Or until the wire suddenly snaps. . . .

Jim Maclaine becomes tired and disillusioned and sick of his fame and lack of privacy and eventually decides, as he has decided so many times in the past, to opt out – for a time at any rate. But can he ever gather the courage and strength and confidence to 'opt in' again? That's the dramatic question posed towards the conclusion of this remarkable and powerful motion picture.

Stardust is made on locations in London, Manchester, Spain and the United States.

SYNOPSIS

Five years ago Jim Maclaine (David Essex) opted out of a potential academic career when he suddenly walked out of the Sixth Form of his local grammar school, left home, and worked as a deck chair attendant as a seaside resort. Later, during casual work at a holiday camp and a fairground, he made friends with Mike Menarry (Adam Faith) but never saw him again after Mike received a severe beating-up from a gang of Teddy-boys. After returning home and tasting the – to him – boring and quiet domestic backwaters of marriage and fatherhood, he deserted his family and bought a guitar with his last few pounds, hoping to find a new career in rock music, which he had come to love.

Now Jim is a member of a small-time touring pop-group called The Stray Cats comprising the leader, Johnny (Paul

Nicholas), J. D. Clover (Keith Moon), Alex (Dave Edmunds) and Stevie (Karl Howman). The time: November, 1963, when the world has been shattered with the news of President Kennedy's assassination.

Jim discovers that Mike is working at the local fairground when The Stray Cats arrive for a local engagement. He asks Mike to join the group as road-manager, realising that Mike's no-nonsense approach and his shrewd mind might be an asset. Mike accepts and almost at once closes an advantageous deal with the manager of the club the group is playing that night. He also warns Jim against Johnny, whom he has quickly summed up as a 'loser'.

Within a few months The Stray Cats are being managed by Ronald Harrap (John Normington), a dapper bachelor who has made a fortune from launderettes and is now investing in the group, more or less as a pastime. It was Mike who originally brought Harrap and the group together and Mike is now an integral and invaluable key-member of the team. It is Harrap who introduces the group to Colin Day (Marty Wilde), head of Dayray Ltd. who, after arranging for The Stray Cats to record a demo-disc (with Jim singing on one side) and being impressed with it, buys out Harrap to handle The Stray Cats himself. The record becomes No. 1 in the charts in Britain and does well in America too, making a star of Jim and, to a lesser degree of the group. Johnny has been 'eased out' and replaced by Kevin (Peter Duncan). By the time they come top in a nationwide poll of pop-stars, Jim Maclaine and The Stray Cats are among the biggest stars in Britain and, after wildly successfully tours, in the United States too.

During appearances in New York, Porter Lee Austin (Larry Hagman) introduces himself to Jim as his new manager; Colin Day has sold out 75% of Stray Cats Incorporated to Austin without bothering to tell Jim. With Austin is his attorney and ever-present associate Felix Hoffman (Rick Lee Parmentier). Jim is astonished at the sudden turn of events but has to reconcile himself to the facts – especially as Austin seems to be a pretty smart operator anyway. Austin lines up a punishing touring schedule for Jim and the group throughout the States and they become bigger stars than ever before.

Jim has now acquired a girl-friend for himself. She is a lovely French girl named Danielle (Ines des Longchamps), who is adoring, loyal – and sometimes troubled at the pressures Jim is being subjected to. By the summer of 1967, Jim and the group, with Austin and the rest of their retinue, are holidaying in Bermuda. After a stormy dinner-party, when Jim loses his temper because Austin expects too much of him, Mike comes in with a message: Jim's mother has died back in England.

Jim, Danielle and Mike fly to England to attend Mrs Maclaine's funeral, which is upset when Jim is swamped with fans and eager Press-men. At the funeral Jim meets his wife Jeannette (Rosalind Ayres), his five year old son Jimmy, and Brian (James Hazeldine), who now lives with Jeannette. Danielle is upset because Jim has never told her of his early marriage.

When Jim returns to the States he learns that The Stray Cats are splitting up and leaving him. They had been resentful of his 'solo' successes for some time now. Jim persuades Mike to stay with him and continues, of course, to be handled by the indefatigable Austin. Danielle walks out of Jim's life too, when Mike (who has never quite liked her – maybe through jealousy?) 'arranges' for her to discover Jim making love to a 'groupie girl'.

Back in London Mike has pulled off a remarkable coup: the first concert performance of Jim Maclaine's *Symphony to Woman* – called *Dea Sancta et Gloria* and based on a few phrases in the Funeral Mass for his mother – is to be televised throughout the world by satellite, with the album going on sale simultaneously. The result is spectacular and, as it turns out, the peak of Jim's meteoric career.

For, despite the fact that he is now the biggest name in the international pop world, Jim has now had enough of it all; the sweet taste of success has turned bitter in his mouth. True to his nature he wants nothing more than to opt out of everything and everyone – everyone, that is, except Mike, on whom he has to come to rely more and more. Jim and Mike go to Spain, where Jim buys a deserted, partly-ruined, small old castle in the wilds of the mountains. He spends a fortune on modernising the interiors and moves in with Mike, who buys a dog. Over the next 18 months the idyllicism wears off and Jim becomes more and more restless and unhappy, even to the point of becoming jealous of Mike's dog. To alleviate the boredom they stage a boxing tournament one night – which Mike wins.

Austin and Hoffman arrive one day and try to persuade Jim to at least make a partial return to the pop world. But Jim believes that his creative juices have dried up. Mike thinks that Jim secretly wants to return. 'He didn't become what he is because he was that much more talented than anyone else. He did it because he wanted to be more famous than anybody else. And he still does,' Mike says. Jim, looking pale, ill and disillusioned, eventually agrees to do an important live television interview at the castle.

But events take an unexpected and dramatic turn. . . .

THE CAST
DAVID ESSEX – JIM MACLAINE

David Essex was born in Plaistow, East London, on July 23, 1947, and educated at Custom House School, by the side of the River Thames. He was interested in music from an early age and when he happened to glance into a music shop window one day, it changed his life. He saw a drum-kit and persuaded his docker father to buy it for him. At 14 he joined a blues band and was seen singing and playing drums in an East End public house by the man who is now his manager, who asked him if he would like a solo career. David said yes and left the band. After making a few single records and appearing in various TV shows, he joined a stage repertory company and toured many theatres throughout Britain. Later came further work on TV, on radio and on stage, including a season in pantomime. He made his film debut in 1970 in *Assault* and later appeared in *All Coppers Are*. Then in November, 1971, came the show which brought stardom and rave reviews: *God-*

spell which opened in London's Roundhouse, later transferring to the West End's Wyndham's Theatre, where it is still running, though David left the cast after two years in the autumn of 1973. He obtained a special leave of absence from the show in the autumn of 1972 to star in *That'll Be The Day*, which was one of the hit films of 1973. It also won David Essex the Variety Club of Great Britain's Most Promising Newcomer of the Year Award, a Nomination in the same category in the Society of Film and Television Arts Awards, announced in March, 1974, and Disc's Award as the Brightest Hope for 1974. David has recently scored major successes with two hit single records – *Rock On* and *Lamplight* (both of which won Silver Discs in the UK). The single of *Rock On* also climbed high in the Top Ten in America and was a big hit in France, too.

David recently completed two highly-successful promotional tours of the United States, plus visits to France, Germany and Holland. David Essex has dark-brown hair, dark-blue eyes, is 5ft 10½ins tall and weighs 10st 3 lbs. He loves horse-riding and playing soccer and was at one time thinking of taking up the game as a career. He lives in the Romford area of Essex. In *Stardust* he again plays the central role of Jim Maclaine (originally introduced in *That'll Be The Day*) who is now a member of an obscure pop group, but who rises to become a top rock superstar of the 1960s, only to opt out at the height of his fame when he finds success can also mean punishing hard work, exhaustion, boredom and disillusionment.

ADAM FAITH – Mike Menarry

Adam Faith was born on June 23, 1940, in London. His real name was Terry Nelhams. His early ambition was to become a film editor and he entered the film industry in the cutting-rooms of Pinewood Studios in 1956, later becoming an assistant editor at Beaconsfield Studios in 1958. He also began singing with a pop group called The Worried Men which played around the coffee bars of London's Soho. He later turned solo, at Jack Good's suggestion, and made his TV debut in Good's *Oh Boy* followed by regular appearances in such TV pop shows as *The 6.5 Special*, *Drumbeat* and *Boy Meets Girls*. *The Adam Faith Show* scored a success in TV when Adam had enjoyed spectacular hits with such top-selling records as *What Do You Want?*, *Poor Me*, *Someone Else's Baby*, *Made You*, *How About That*, *Lonely Pup* and *The Time Has Come* between 1959–61. He made his motion picture bow in *Beat Girl* in 1959 and his subsequent films include *Never Let Go*, *What A Whopper* and *Mix Me A Person*.

During the early sixties he topped variety bills in theatres all over Britain, appeared regularly in TV shows and on radio, appeared in a Royal Command Performance, starred in summer shows and in pantomime. During the late sixties, Adam played the lead in several stage productions, improving his acting technique with every performance; among his appearances were those in theatre productions of *Night Must Fall*, *Billy Liar*, *Alfie*, *Pickwick* and *Twelfth Night*. In 1970 he scored an enormous success in the title-role of the TV series *Budgie*, in which he played a likeable small-time crook who was forever hoping to make the criminal 'big-time'. Two years ago Adam Faith discovered Leo Sayer (currently on the way to the top as a British pop star) and now manages him and produces his records.

Adam was seriously injured in a car-crash in August, 1973, and it was several months before he fully recovered. He has recently recorded an album of songs which he co-wrote with David Courtney and which will be issued soon.

Now Adam Faith returns to films with *Stardust*, in which he is seen as Mike Menarry, an old friend of Jim Maclaine's whom he now helps to the top of the pop ladder in his capacity as Jim's cynical, sardonic and perceptive personal manager. Adam and his wife Jackie now live in Sussex with their small daughter Katya.

KEITH MOON – J. D. CLOVER
Keith Moon was born in London in 1947 and educated at Harrow Technical College, Middlesex. On leaving school he

worked as a trainee electrician and part-time newspaper delivery boy in Wembley, also playing the drums in his spare time with a group called The Beachcombers. One day he saw the recently formed group The Who as a member of their audience and asked if he could sit-in with them on drums. Pete Townshend, Roger Daltrey and John Entwistle were so impressed that, at 17, they invited him to join them as the group's permanent drummer. That was in 1964 and The Who's subsequent rise to fame and fortune is now a show business legend. Their first big hit was *I Can't Explain*, followed by such records as *Anyway, Anyhow, Anywhere, My Generation, Substitute, I'm A Boy, Happy Jack, Pictures of Lily, I Can See for Miles* and *Pinball Wizard*. Their massive double-albums of their rock operas *Tommy* (soon to be filmed by Ken Russell) and *Quadrophenia* have received acclaim, as have their own live performances of these remarkable works. And always on the centre of the stage with The Who is drummer Keith Moon – 'in every way the perfect rock drummer' as one leading critic recently described him. Keith made his film debut in Frank Zappa's *200 Motels* (as a nun!) and has since appeared in *Count Downe* and *That'll Be The Day*. He lives in a highly-futuristic house in Chertsey, Surrey. In *Stardust* he plays J. D. Clover, the talented, zany drummer with Jim Maclaine's group The Stray Cats.

MARTY WILDE – COLIN DAY

Marty Wilde was born on April 15th, 1939, in Greenwich, South London. In 1958, whilst singing (under his real name) as Reg Smith and the Hound Dogs at a London club, he was spotted by impresario Larry Parnes, who changed his name and signed him to a contract. Parnes booked him into London's famous night club Winston's, where Josephine Douglas, producer of the popular BBC TV pop show *The 6.5 Special* saw him. She booked him for the show and he was an immediate hit. He was soon making chart-topping records, the first of which was *Endless Sleep* in 1958. Subsequent hits include *Donna, Teenager in Love, Sea of Love, Bad Boy, Little Girl,*

Rubber Ball and *Jezebel*. He toured with his own group The Wild Cats and was voted Number Two British Pop Singer of 1958. In 1959 he was one of the stars of Jack Good's popular TV show *Oh Boy*; one of the other stars was Adam Faith, who also appears in *Stardust*.

In 1959, too, Marty Wilde made his film debut in *Jet Storm*, and his subsequent films include *The Hellions* and *What A Crazy World*. In more recent years Marty has written many hit songs, include *Jesamine, Ice In The Sun, Abergavenny* and, for Lulu, *I'm A Tiger*. He also wrote the musical version of Alun Owen's famous television play *No Trams To Lime Street*, which was seen on TV and also on a provincial stage tour. As well as his successful song-writing, Marty has made many cabaret appearances and also toured in the recent sell-out touring *74 Rock 'n' Roll Road Show*. His son is the teeny-bop heart-throb record-star Ricky Wilde. In *Stardust* he plays Colin Day the first big-time manager-agent to The Stray Cats group.

PAUL NICHOLAS – JOHNNY

Paul Nicholas was born in 1945 in Peterborough, and educated in London. On leaving school he worked for his father, a well-known London solicitor. Then, as a piano-player, he toured extensively, both in England and in Europe with a successful pop group. In 1968 he starred as Claude in the West End production of *Hair*. He also appeared in the BBC TV play *The Season Of The Witch* with Robert Powell. He made his motion picture bow in *Cannabis* with Jane Birkin, subsequently playing the killer in *Blind Terror* opposite Mia Farrow and the leading role of Jack in *Whatever Happened to Jack and Jill*. He next returned to *Hair* as artistic director until he opened in the title-role of *Jesus Christ, Superstar* at London's Palace Theatre in 1972. In 1973 he went on to star as Danny Zuko in the London production of the rock-show *Grease*. In *Stardust* he plays Johnny, the original leader of The Stray Cats group – until he is later eased out by Jim Maclaine.

INES DES LONGCHAMPS – Danielle

Ines des Longchamps was born on March 16th, 1950, in Paris, and is the daughter of a prominent French diplomat. Since her father's duties take him all over the world, Ines received her education in Vietnam, Spain, Ethiopia, Morocco and Sweden, ending up with a spell at a finishing-school in Italy. She is currently in her fourth year at a drama school in Paris and has appeared in one stage production there. She makes her screen debut in *Stardust*, in which she plays Danielle, Jim Maclaines' beautiful and loyal girl-friend, who becomes increasingly troubled at the pressures he has to bear when he becomes a top rock superstar of the 1960s. Ines lives in Paris.

THE PRODUCTION TEAM
DAVID PUTTNAM

David Puttnam was born in London in 1941, and educated at Minchenden Grammar School in North London, leaving at the age of 17 to join a leading advertising agency. By the time he was 23, he had become the youngest account controller in advertising with Collett, Dickenson, Pearce & Partners, handling over three-million dollars of billings per annum. Two years later, at the age of 25, David Puttnam started his own company, David Puttnam Associates, photographers agents, which within two years became the largest company of its type in the world, with an annual turnover in excess of 750,000 dollars. After three years he became concerned at the limited long term growth potential of the business, and at the same time was fascinated by the potential of cassette television. As a result, together with Sanford Lieberson, he formed Visual Programme Systems Ltd. To facilitate this move and allow him to devote his attention to the cassette market, David Puttnam reduced his holding in David Puttnam Associates to 60%, took a non-executive position as chairman with the company and moved it to separate premises, although he still maintains a close interest in the company's activities. As well as being deeply involved with VPS, David Puttnam has ventured into film production through Goodtimes Enterprises. In 1969/70 he developed and produced *Melody* starring Mark Lester and Jack Wild. This was followed in 1971 by *The Pied Piper of Hamelin*, directed by Jacques Demy and starring Donovan, Jack Wild, Donald Pleasance and John Hurt. In 1972 he produced (with Sandy Lieberson) *That'll Be The Day*. In 1973 he was executive co-producer (with Roy Baird) of *The Final Programme*, starring Jon Finch; also (with Sandy Lieberson) of Ken Russell's *Mahler*. The same year he co-produced (with Sandy Lieberson) *The Double-headed Eagle* and *Swastika*. David Puttnam firmly believes that his marketing background gives him an enormous advantage in conceiving and producing saleable product in the currently highly volatile and changing TV and film business.

SANDY LIEBERSON

Sandy Lieberson was born in California in 1936 and educated at the Los Angeles City College. He started his career in public relations, handling such diverse accounts as the Public Health Division of the State of California, the Diners Club and rock 'n' roll star Little Richard. He then moved into the film and theatrical agency field with the William Morris Agency, working as assistant to the company president. Following this he came to Europe for the Grade Organisation, working in Paris, London, and in particular, Rome: his knowledge of both the European and American market led to his appointment as managing director of the London office of Creative Management Associates, the largest and one of the most highly regarded agencies in the world. This position involved handling the company's operations in Europe, and in fact Sanford Lieberson was operative in setting up a branch of CMA in Rome and appointing representatives in other major cities. His responsibilities covered not only the handling of clients such as Peter Sellers, Barbra Streisand, The Rolling Stones, Richard Harris, Anouk Aimee, etc., but also the TV syndication in the UK and Europe of all CMA television product, including the CBS Barbra Streisand TV Specials and various other big television shows. He specialised in representing European and British producers for overseas markets, and acting as agent in setting up various Franco-Italian co-productions with American financing, including the setting up of Universal Pictures Ltd's first Franco-Italian co-production. In 1968, Sanford Lieberson left CMA to become a producer, forming his own company of Goodtimes Enterprises Ltd. His first film was *Performance* for Warner Bros. He also acted as executive producer on the Rolling Stones' Rock 'N' Roll TV Special.

Realising the potential of the cassette market and the growing interest in it, he went ahead in 1969 to form Visual Programme Systems with David Puttnam, incorporating Goodtimes Enterprises into the structure of their partnership. In 1972 he produced (with David Puttnam) *That'll Be The Day*. In 1973 he co-produced (with John Goldstone) *The Final Programme*, starring Jon Finch, and was also executive co-producer (with David Puttnam) of Ken Russell's *Mahler*. The same year he co-produced (with David Puttnam) *The Double-Headed Eagle* and *Swastika*.

ROY BAIRD – EXECUTIVE PRODUCER

Roy Baird was born in Borehamwood, Hertfordshire, in 1933 and educated at the Norwich City College. He always had ambitions to enter the film industry and, after two years' National Service in the RAF as a technical writer, he became a third assistant director. A year later he became a second asistant, and a year after that a first assistant. For the next three years he worked mainly in television as both a first assistant director and a director of second units. He then worked as assistant director on feature films made by The Boulting Brothers, Val Guest, Sidney Fury and William Wyler (on *The Collector*). He next became production manager on Karel Reisz's film *Morgan: A Suitable Case For Treatment* and assistant director to John Huston on *Casino Royale*. Then came a step up to associate producer on Jack Clayton's *Our Mother's House*, after which he joined Albert Finney's company, Memorial Enterprises, as an executive producer, working in this capacity on *If . . .* and *Spring And Port Wine*. He subsequently became associate producer on Ken Russell's *Women In Love*, remaining with Russell's production company to work as executive producer on *The Music Lovers* and as associate producer on the controversial *The Devils*. In 1971 he produced the highly successful film *Henry VIII And His Six Wives*, in 1972 was executive producer of *That'll Be The Day*, and in 1973 was executive producer (with David Puttnam) of *The Final Programme*, all three films being for Anglo-EMI. In 1973 he produced Ken Russell's *Mahler*, for Goodtimes Enterprises Productions.

MICHAEL APTED – THE DIRECTOR

Michael Apted was born on February 10th, 1941, in Aylesbury, Buckinghamshire. After studying history and law at Cambridge University, he joined Granada Television as a trainee in 1963. After five months he joined the current affairs programme *World In Action* as a researcher, also working on other documentary productions. He later directed *Cinema* and *All Our Yesterdays*. In 1966 he began directing the popular, long-running serial *Coronation Street*, followed by several Granada TV drama productions. In 1969 he left Granada to turn freelance director. His big break came in 1970 when he directed Colin Welland's play *Slatterey's Mounted Foot*, followed by *The Mosedale Horseshoe*, Alun Owen's *Joy*, and the successful comedy series *The Lovers*. He has since directed more than sixty TV plays including, most notably, *A £1,000 For Rosebud*, *Another Sunday and Sweet F.A.*, *Said The Preacher*, *The Reporters*, *Buggins Ermine*, *Kisses at Fifty*, *Jack Point* and *A Great Day For Bonzo*. In 1971 he directed his first motion picture, the widely acclaimed *The Triple Echo* starring Glenda Jackson and Oliver Reed. Now comes his second film *Stardust*. Michael Apted lives in Teddington, Middlesex, with his wife, Jo, and their seven year old son, Paul. In his spare time he is a keen football fan and has been a West Ham supporter since he was eight years old.

RAY CONNOLLY – THE WRITER

Ray Connolly was born in 1940 in St. Helen's, Lancashire, and educated at St. Helen's Catholic Grammar School. He then read anthropology for three years at the London School of Economics, gaining his B.Sc. (Soc.) degree. During his time at the LSE he co-edited, wrote for and published a glossy film magazine titled *Motion*, which achieved a minor success, especially in London and other movie-conscious cities. He also wrote for other publications and eventually joined *The Liverpool Daily Post* in 1966 as a sub-editor, but was disappointed because they wouldn't let him write. When he was put in charge of the features pages he solved this problem by doing interviews with local celebrities during the day and publishing them on the features pages at night – under different names! He sent samples of his work to the London *Evening Standard*, who invited him to join them. His popular, influential and widely-read Saturday interview page in this paper ran from 1967 until the end of 1973 when he left for a sabbatical to concentrate on other work. His first novel, *A Girl Who Came To Stay*, was published in 1973. He wrote the screenplay for the successful *That'll Be The Day* in 1972. The film came tenth in the top money-making motion pictures in the UK for 1973.

Now comes Connolly's *Stardust*, which continues the story of Jim Maclaine (again played by David Essex). Connolly's paper-back novelisation of *That'll Be The Day* was also a success. Ray Connolly lives in Kensington with his wife Plum and their three children: Louise (6), Dominic (4) and Kieron (1).

APPENDIX IV
Quotations on the *Stardust* set

Here are some of the quotations attributed to David Essex while he was working on his latest film *Stardust*: —

'Early on, when I was playing drums in a blues group in East End pubs and clubs, I became the singer as well — because mine was the only voice that had broken....'

*

'Remembering what I was and what I could have become is the best way I know of keeping my sanity.'

*

'At this moment in my career I'm being swept along on a wave — but I'm still managing to steer the ship. I'll only do the things that I believe in.'

*

'I'm an entertainer not an intellectual.'

*

'I've discovered that happiness comes from good work rather than big cheques.'

*

'I've got a pride in my work, that's the one big driving-force inside me.'

*

'Today I would describe myself as a rock-singer, a rock-actor, and a rock-musician. The rock bit is very important to me and always has been.'

'I like having fans. It's a mark of success. If I could walk down the street without being surrounded by a gang of fans, I'd be worried.'

*

'When I was a kid in the East End of London, a crowd of us used to play Russian Roulette with a packet of Woodbine's cigarettes. We'd all sit round and chain-smoke and the first kid to be sick was out. . . .'

*

'People often see me as a rebel because I go my own way. But if I didn't I'd feel dishonest.'

*

'I don't like being compared to other stars such as James Dean. I want to be the first David Essex. No one can have a great career who just follows a star. . . .'

*

'Jim Maclaine, the character I play in *Stardust*, becomes a superstar. I don't particularly want to become a superstar myself. I'm more interested in getting respect for the music I play.'

*

'I don't really like much of what I do. I'm extremely self-critical.'

*

'I'll always remember my time in *Godspell* as being among the happiest times of my life.'

*

'I can really identify with the Jim Maclaine character. But not all the way. . . .'

*

'I try and get along with people, but I hate blokes who put their arms around your shoulder and call you "luv" . . .'

'Am I rich? I wouldn't know. The money talked about is like Monopoly money. It's so much it isn't real.'

*

'I feel very loyal and thankful towards fans because they've always been very good to me. It's also a mistake to talk or write down to fans. Not enough artists give them credit for having enough intelligence. As far as I'm concerned, they're great!'

*

'I know I've got talent, but I won't know how much unless I keep testing myself and extending the things I do.'

*

'If it all packed up on me I could easily go back to a job like lorry-driving. . . .'